Essays on Earl Renfroe— A Man of Firsts

Edited by William S. Bike

D1598627

Index

Foreword: A Legacy of Achievement

by Bruce S. Graham, DDS, MS, MEd
Dean, University of Illinois at Chicago
(UiC) College of Dentistry

In the 1920s, the University of Illinois at Chicago College of Dentistry began attracting individuals who dreamed big dreams, and who went on to achieve great accomplishments. These were dentists who were the first to achieve various teaching and research accomplishments in their fields, and who led their students and their colleagues to even greater attainments.

One of dentistry's great achievers, whom for 70 years the College was privileged to call its own, was Dr. Earl Wiley Renfroe.

Dr. Renfroe made history in several areas—aeronautics and the military among them. But it is his pathbreaking work at the College of Dentistry that makes those of us affiliated with the College most proud.

Earl Renfroe was the first student at the College to work full-time while carrying a full course load. Despite this burden, he graduated first in his class of 127 in 1931.

Named an instructor in oral diagnosis at the College in 1933, Dr. Renfroe, after earning his master's in orthodontics at the College in 1942, joined the orthodontics faculty in 1946.

As a teacher, Dr. Renfroe was called "prolific," "an inspiration," and "one of the best orthodontic teachers in the world" by students. Typical is a comment by Dr. Stanley Rosenthal: "...whatever caliber of clinical orthodontist graduated was entirely due to [Dr. Renfroe's] patience and skill...."

The students that he mentored during the six decades in which he taught here have gone on not only to spread the renown of the UIC College of Dentistry through their skill and acumen, but have enabled the College to create a far-reaching, positive impact on the public's oral health.

Not content to educate only American orthodontic students, Dr. Renfroe   onsidered one of

1

Dr. Earl Renfroe at the UIC College of Dentistry in the early 1960s.

the fathers of orthodontics in Brazil and was invited to lecture there seven times—a unique honor for an American dentist. In Barbados, Dr. Renfroe was honored with the naming of a dental facility for him.

With fellow faculty member Dr. Thomas K. Barber from the Department of Pediatric Dentistry, he wrote a seminal clinical article that in 1957 helped create the field of preventive and interceptive orthodontics.

As chief of the U.S. Army's Dental Service at Ft. Huachuca, Arizona, during World War II, Dr. Renfroe's reorganization of the service gained the favorable attention of the military high command. He remained in the U.S. Army Reserves thereafter, retiring as a colonel in 1968 and being awarded the rank of brigadier general in the Illinois Army National Guard in 1984.

Dr. Renfroe also was a great achiever in breaking the boundaries of racial prejudice. In 1934, he became the first Illinoisan of African-American heritage to be licensed as a commercial airplane pilot. In 1950, he became the first African-American dentist to open a new practice in Chicago's Loop since the 1880s, and the first African-American orthodontist to do so. Through Dr. Renfroe's efforts, the College began the policy of dentists providing care to patients without regard to race. And in 1966, his being named head of the Department of Orthodontics made him the first African-American to lead a department at the College.

A pathbreaker in clinical orthodontic teaching, aeronautics, military organization, international dentistry, and race relations, Dr. Renfroe has left a legacy of accomplishments that have benefited the public while enhancing the reputation of the College of Dentistry worldwide.

For these and other successes, he has earned a special place in the College's Kottemann Gallery of Dentistry, which tells the story of the impact the College has had on dentistry and the world. That story would not be complete, nor nearly as interesting, without Dr. Earl Renfroe, who lived a life of triumph that benefitted all.

The UIC College of Dentistry stresses teaching, research, and public service. Those goals also can sum up Dr. Renfroe's incredibly influential life.

I was fortunate to have met Dr. Renfroe and his wife, Hilda, in 2000. I spent time with them in the home they shared with their son, Stephen; their daughter-in-law, Cheryl; and their grandchildren, Chase and Julie. It was a wonderful experience. I am thankful to the family for the opportunity to get to know, however, briefly, one of dentistry's all-time greats.

Some who will read this book were his students; some were his colleagues; some are family; some knew him briefly; and some know him only by reputation. Some experienced firsthand his passion for teaching, his commitment to any student who came to him for guidance, and his incredible hands-on orthodontic skill.

All live in a better world because of a man who was an achiever in so many venues: Dr. Earl Wiley Renfroe.

(Left to right) Former UIC College of Dentistry Dean Allen Anderson with Dr. Earl Renfroe and UIC President James Stukel, celebrating the opening of a new orthodontics clinic at College of Dentistry.

An Abridged Biographical Sketch of Dr. Earl Wiley Renfroe

by Claude E. Driskell, DDS
University of Illinois at Chicago College of Dentistry
Class of 1954

Dr. Earl Wiley Renfroe was born January 9, 1907, on the Southeast Side of Chicago, Illinois. His middle name, Wiley, was his mother's maiden name.

Dr. Renfroe was married from 1942 until they passed away in 2000 to the former Hilda Forte, who hailed from Barbados. Dr. and Mrs. Renfroe had two children, Diane and Stephen, and Dr. Renfroe had a son, Earl Jr., from a previous marriage.

His family background typifies the integrated lifestyle as much as our society for most of the 20th century permitted. Dr. Renfroe's youth was spent in all-white southeast Chicago, and later in all-white Woodlawn, during the first few decades of the 20th century. His brother, Everett, was one of the first licensed radio operators in the world, and his sister, Hazel, was an art instructor who had received her training at the Sorbonne in Paris.

Between 1913 and 1921 Earl Renfroe was enrolled at Austin O. Sexton Grammar School at 641 E. 60th St.—the only African-American child in his class.

"Only" or "first" status would be his throughout his whole life experience, which carried him forth to become the "first" African-American in countless endeavors.

From 1921 to 1925, Earl attended James H. Bowen High School, again as the lone African-American in his class. There, he also became the first African-American student in the school's history to attain the rank of Cadet Commander in its Reserve Officers Training Corps (ROTC).

He then moved on to Crane Junior College, and in 1927 he was accepted to the University of Illinois College of Dentistry in Chicago. And after successfully completing his four professional

Young Earl Renfroe (with saxophone) with his brother, Everett, and sister, Hazel.

years of dental training with academic honors, he graduated as a dentist with a Doctor of Dental Surgery degree in 1931.

A year later, Dr. Renfroe received his professional license to practice general dentistry in Illinois, which he did until 1940. While practicing general dentistry, Dr. Renfroe was appointed as a part-time instructor in the Oral Diagnosis Clinic of the College of Dentistry, serving in that role from 1933 to 1935.

The 1930s were a busy time for Dr. Renfroe. In 1932, he joined the Illinois National Guard. Two years later, he became the first African-American in Illinois (and only the third in the nation) to obtain a commercial pilot's license. He later served as an inspector for the Illinois Aeronautics Commission.

From 1935 until 1940, he held the rank of instructor in the College's infirmary. At that time, the teacher decided to go back to being a student in the College of Dentistry, this time for specialty training. Two years later, he received a Master of Science degree in the specialty of orthodontics from the College. Upon

Earl Renfroe (front row, far right) was the only African-American in the A.O. Sexton School's eighth grade class of 1921.

Earl Renfroe's decades-long career in the U.S. Army Reserves lasted until 1968, when he retired as a colonel. In 1984, the State of Illinois honored him for his military service by naming him a brigadier general in the Illinois National Guard.

receiving his certification, he officially became the first black dentist in Chicago to become an orthodontist.

Called into military service after his earning his master's in orthodontics in 1942, Dr. Renfroe quickly rose to the rank of Lieutenant Colonel, the highest rank attained up to that time by an African-American dental officer in the U.S. Army, and served as Chief of the Dental Service at Ft. Huachuca, Arizona, from 1943 to 1945. Dr. Renfroe's military career did not end with World War II, as he stayed in the U.S. Army Reserves, retiring as a colonel in 1968. The State of Illinois in 1984 awarded him the rank of general in the Illinois Army National Guard.

Dr. Renfroe returned to the College of Dentistry in 1946 to become an instructor in the graduate school's orthodontic clinic. The next year, he became an assistant professor in orthodontics. At the same time, he opened a dental office as an orthodontist on the South Side. As his practice grew, Dr. Renfroe saw the need in 1950 to move downtown to an office at 127 N. Dearborn, becoming not only the first black orthodontist in the Loop but, Dr. Renfroe asserted, the first acknowledged black professional in any field in Chicago's downtown at that time, other than a light-complected African-American dentist whom most people assumed was white.

Concerning orthodontics, once again, he led a trend. According to Dr. Renfroe, the 1940s and 1950s saw a phenomenal increase in the public's demand for orthodontic services, as radio and television helped to elevate the "dental IQ" of the general public.

In June of 1950, after waiting 19 years since his graduation from the College of Dentistry as the highest academically ranked student in his class, he was at last admitted into the once-segregated honors society Omicron Kappa Upsilon (OKU), putting another nail in the coffin of Jim Crow.

In 1953 Dr. Renfroe was promoted to associate professor, and four years later he was elevated to the esteemed rank of full professor, lecturing to juniors from 1963 to 1966 and to freshmen from 1968 to 1972. When Dr. Renfroe accepted the rank of professor, his increased workload at the College necessitated his

Dr. Earl Renfroe, chairman of the Department of Orthodontics at the UIC College of Dentistry, 1966.

cutting down his private orthodontic practice hours, at some considerable financial sacrifice.

The professor did, however, find the time to author a landmark textbook, *Technique Training in Orthodontics*, which was published in 1960.

Dr. Renfroe eclipsed all of his previous honors in 1966 when he was named head of the Department of Orthodontics—the first African-American head of a department at the UIC College of Dentistry. He was an appropriate successor in that post to Dr. Allan G. Brodie Sr., considered to be one of the founding fathers of orthodontics.

Only a year later, Dr. Renfroe was invited to become head of the Department of Graduate Orthodontics at the dental college of the College of Physicians and Surgeons in San Francisco, but he turned it down (as he also turned down an opportunity to head an orthodontics department at a Brazilian dental school), electing to stay at UIC.

There, he held the rank of professor and head through 1973. In 1972-73 he also served on the medical staff of the University of Illinois Hospital. After his retirement in 1973, Dr. Renfroe held the rank of professor emeritus, and beginning in 1982 and continuing for several years, he once again became very active as a volunteer in the orthodontics department.

His short time in retirement was not an era of inaction, however, as another pathbreaking orthodontics textbook of his, *Edgewise*, was published in English in 1975, and in Japanese in 1977.

Dr. Renfroe's accomplishments as a dentist, an aviator, and a military man were unsurpassed, but yet they were not enough for this Renaissance man. He belonged to ten professional organizations in dentistry, including the Chicago Association of Orthodontists, which he served as president, 1963-64.

His wide range of interests—particularly his hobbies of amateur radio operation, pistol and rifle marksmanship, model locomotives, and SCUBA diving—saw him active in over a dozen civic organizations. The eclectic mix included the Chicago Council on Foreign Relations (which he served as vice president in 1968); the Chicago Urban League; the Chicago Natural History (now Field) Museum; the Druids; the International Oceanographic Foundation; the National Conference of Christians and Jews; the National Geographic Society; the 20 Fathom (SCUBA) Club; and many more.

Interest in knowledge for knowledge's sake took him to 30 countries as a traveler, but he was determined to share knowledge, too, as he lectured on orthodontics in nine foreign lands. Among them was Brazil, which honored Dr. Renfroe by making him the first American dentist to be invited back seven times.

A man of stellar reputation, Dr. Renfroe also appeared in eight published "Who's Whos," such as *Who's Who in the World*, the *Blue Book of London*, and *American Men of Science*. In 1988, he was honored with the Distinguished Alumnus Award by the UIC Dental Alumni Association, and two years later, he was inducted in to the Chicago Senior Citizens Hall of Fame.

Through it all, wrote author Lerone Bennett in *Ebony* magazine in March 1955, Dr. Renfroe was "an earnest, plain-spoken man who approaches his work with the zeal of a missionary and the skill of an artist." He stated that Dr. Renfroe "fearlessly treads out into the deep, uncharted waters never challenged or explored before when he challenges and confronts racism...."

Dr. Renfroe's willingness to take on racism paid off. During the decade of the 1970s, he stated, the distribution of black orthodontists became greater than ever before. He said that in Chicago alone, five or six black dentists were practicing the specialty of orthodontics, a number that a few years earlier would have been a large one for the entire United States.

Because of his accomplishments, the UIC College of Dentistry is working to establish an endowed chair in Dr. Renfroe's name. There is no higher tribute in academe, and no more fitting tribute possible for Earl Wiley Renfroe, the man of firsts.

Editor's note: Dr. Renfroe's full curriculum vitae can be found later in the book.

The Times of Dr. Earl Wiley Renfroe

by Claude E. Driskell, DDS
University of Illinois at Chicago College of Dentistry
Class of 1954

1. The American Scene Through the 19th Century

To better comprehend the exploits of Earl Wiley Renfroe, one must also review the changes that society had undergone when he arrived upon the American scene.

Young, developing America, comprised of races, cultures, and religions from all over the world, during the 19th century had divided into a modern manufacturing/industrial North, and a more outdated agricultural South, for many years maintained by slave labor—making the American Union a half-slave, half-free house divided.

But the 19th century also was an era of enlightenment and transformation, birthing a completely altered, more democratic world. And with the rise of industrial cities in the Northern states, thousands of poor Southern whites and fugitive (and later free) slaves migrated there seeking greater hope and a better life.

That century possessed the strong shoulders upon which the 20th century was founded, marking a time in which the old ways of the past reluctantly succumbed to the new. That new century evolved as a very different place from any that had been known before; through enlightened consciousness, it eradicated many traditional ignorances, fears, and mysteries that had previously overshadowed progress.

When freedom came to the American slaves, a small but able and competent group of educated and literate black leaders came forth to guide a lost mass of freed, but frustrated and confused, people into life as American citizens. These leaders had their work cut out for them—as ninety percent of the ex-slaves were illiterate, and they still faced the opposition of the former slave-master class.

Three black leaders stand out in the post-Emancipation era:

Dr. Renfroe was an important pioneer in the history of Chicago. The city recognized his accomplishments by inducting him into its Senior Citizens Hall of Fame, for which he received the congratulations of Mayor Richard M. Daley.

Frederick Douglass (1817-1895); Booker T. Washington (1856-1915); and William E. B. Du Bois (1868-1963).

Douglas was an escaped slave who later purchased his freedom and became an abolitionist and journalist. During the Civil War, he recruited blacks for the North, and during Reconstruction he pressed for black rights.

Washington, born to a Virginia slave family, was an educator who urged industrial education as the path to economic independence. He favored racial cooperation rather than political action.

Du Bois, another educator, helped transform blacks' view of their role in America. A hero to black intellectuals, he was a professor of economics, history, and, finally, head of the sociology department at Atlanta University.

Emancipation had a direct impact on Chicago, as the city's black population grew from 955 in 1860, to 3,691 by 1870, to 30,150 by 1900. After World War I opened up the job market, helping cause the great migrational exodus of blacks from the Deep South, the black population grew to 109,458 by 1920. World War II had a similar effect, and from 1940 to 1950 Chicago's black population grew from 277,731 to 492,265, with 96 percent of that increase due to the influx of poor Southern Blacks. By 1980, Chicago's black population was 1,187,600.

The Renfroe family was part of that great exodus—Earl's father had migrated from Tennessee to Chicago's South Side in the late 19th century. (His mother had come from Galliopolis, Ohio.)

Chicago's South and West Sides have had extremely strong and intimate Southern ties since the end of the Civil War. Transplanted Southerners and descendants sometimes call Chicago's black communities the "suburbs" of the Deep South.

The slower-paced, less educated Southern black migrants often strongly resisted the lifestyle of the new industrialized urban setting, often retaining much of their Southern and rural culture, religion, customs, diet, language, mannerisms, and social behavior. The massive immigration of these individuals therefore changed the customs, atmosphere, and environment of the city's original black community. For one example, there was less emphasis placed on formal higher education.

As the city's black population almost doubled between 1950 and 1960, the business center of the South Side "black belt" shifted from 47th Street to 63rd Street. Thousands of more affluent and more formally educated blacks moved southwards and eastwards into relatively newer attractive homes, vacated by whites. Even the older parts of the black belt developed a new look through extensive slum-clearance, highrises, and rebuilding—although overall, the black belt was still over-crowded and a ghetto to a great extent.

While the city's emerging, expanding, and formally educated black upper class demanded respectable social public behavior, the subculture of the poorer class often prevailed by sheer weight of numbers.

Earl grew up in the southeast corner of Chicago's South Side, which was not only divided by race and ethnicity, but also by class. There were two distinct South Side black communities, with State Street serving as their border. To the east resided the relatively more affluent; to the west, the relatively poorer.

2. The World of Earl Renfroe

Earl Renfroe, having been born in 1907 in the South Side's eastern black community, lived a life spanning almost the entire length of the most tumultuous century in history.

He entered the world only 42 years after the emancipation of African-Americans from slavery, and only 36 years since the famed Chicago Fire and the depression of the 1870s. Although his family had not had much material wealth, his relations constituted an ambitious, achieving African-American family rich in aspirations and desire, and saturated with a wealth of drive and a strong will to excel and achieve. From Earl's earliest days, his parents emphasized the benefits and advantages of a well-directed formal education.

During Earl's youth, his father worked for the U.S. Post Office in Chicago, which provided him with considerable prestige and social status within the black community. At the time, employment at the Post Office was known in the African-American community as "going to college," because of the number of highly educated blacks who worked there. It seemed Jim Crow prevented them from utilizing their educations to achieve higher goals.

Earl Renfroe, too, always progressively sought higher goals, and his life was one of constant growth, development, and almost miraculous evolution to level after level of amazing accomplishments.

Although young Earl also attained employment in the Post Office, he and his parents had greater plans for his future. The

Post Office helped finance his college and professional education, which would help him achieve significant and meaningful accomplishments that made an impact on human history.

3. Young Earl Renfroe's Chicago

In Earl's youth, Chicago still was a relatively young, but progressive, aggressive, and apparently prospering city. Earl witnessed and participated in the experiences of a growing American democratic society attempting to both incorporate and amalgamate multi-cultural, multi-racial, and multi-religious segments, and to create and establish an atmosphere of collective co-existence and compatibility for all concerned.

The Columbian Exposition, or World's Fair of 1893, had left a veneer and a residual belief that a pseudo-boom era was occurring in a city expressing the greatest advances of a growing industrial age and progress to any visiting tourists.

But few visitors to the city really saw its true other side—that of the struggling, ethnically diverse working class; of the poor and underpaid fighting each other for jobs and decent homes in which to rear their respective families.

This competition testified to the social cost of Chicago's pseudo-phenomenal economic and material growth. The depression and industrial strife of the 1870s left thousands of Chicagoans, particularly blacks, jobless. A series of reform ventures was launched, but the problems of industrial strife and corrupt politics that confronted the city's reformers at the turn of the century were complicated by the city's great ethnic diversity, exacerbated by the addition of job-seekers from the American South and from Europe.

By 1920, at least eighty percent of Chicago's population was composed of immigrants from these two areas.

The multi-racial, multi-cultural, and deeply divided nature of the city created a bafflingly complex urban life. Unfamiliar with this and other aspects of Midwestern industrial culture, the new migrants strove against difficult odds to maintain their own ethnic integrity. Chicago was fast developing into many little enclaves.

Winds of change were, however, blowing across the world, forcing away many old prejudices and traditions, unsettling the stability and endurability of old "truths" that once were taken for granted, but were now long overdue to be updated as the collective consciousness became more enlightened and relatively wiser.

The age-old, stagnated way of thinking of a more rigid, materialistic society was gradually giving way in favor of one more charged with stupendous energies and advanced thinking.

4. A Better Future: Not 'Why?', but 'Why Not?'

Dr. Renfroe apparently was one of these gifted, advanced thinkers who saw the world as it was, and felt that it could become much better. But challenging old, established traditions, might have seemed to the less courageous mind to be too premature.

Like the three great challengers before him, Frederick Douglass, Booker T. Washington, and W.E.B. DuBois, Dr. Renfroe accepted the challenges put before him, thinking, "If not me, who else is presently willing?" History has proven that Dr. Renfroe belongs in the same category with these other exalted greats.

The UIC College of Dentistry and its black dental graduates proudly recognize the ambitions, courageous exploits, and achievements of this great leader. In Dr. Renfroe's productive lifetime, he accomplished a host of firsts. He purposefully directed and dedicated his life to helping correct injustices and human rights violations suffered by minorities in dentistry.

Historically, it must also be put on record that America as a nation must be admirably commended as the first civilization in human history to attempt to make a seemingly impossible situation functionally work. Since 1776, it has attempted against all odds and opposition to make a multiplicity of races, cultures, and ethnic groups compatibly co-exist somewhat harmoniously together as a national family.

This national culture, and the political and economic booms and recession periods and their respective effects of Dr. Renfroe's lifetime, along with those of two World Wars, established an atmosphere and environment in which Dr. Renfroe could flourish, although the path would be a difficult one. For superimposed upon these factors that all Americans of the time encountered was his world as a minority in white America.

As he was compelled to grow up under unavoidable social pressures, he took it upon himself to re-invent himself, in spite of the constant pressures of racism.

His remarkable life profoundly proves that if someone has the dedicated, sincere, significant, and meaningful will and directed drive to help change the developmental effects of an apparently and seemingly inevitable and traditional age-old course of events, one can live a life that can retain dignity, self-worth, self-esteem, and self-respect, not only for the sake of personal growth, but for the benefit of society.

We recognize that Dr. Renfroe was not an ordinary man. He always had unique aims, ideals, goals, and aspirations for himself, and always felt restlessly uncomfortable with mediocrity.

Dr. Renfroe felt that he was compelled from within, spiritually, to do something to transform the traditionally segregated and discriminatory conditions he was forced to endure and persevere through during his formative years and school years in Chicago.

Because such courageous, fearless, and intelligent personalities are rare among us, the process of improving African-Americans' human rights and changing the flow of racially imposed circumstances thrust upon them has been painstakingly slow.

Unbeknownst to Dr. Renfroe during the heat of his accomplishments were the pivotally tide-turning and significant marks in human history he would personally imprint during his productive life experience.

We understand them, however, and can greatly appreciate

his firsts in the field of dentistry—made all the more significant by the times in which he achieved them.

We all have had our respective heroes. For people who often have been systematically excluded from the mainstream of American society, it is especially important to remember and celebrate those of us who have won victories and acclaim against tremendous forces arrayed against them.

Dr. Earl Wiley Renfroe is one of those heroes. He shines as a beacon of symbolic hope for the American future. His name and achievements rank with those of the three other historic greats before him—great persons of color who became living proof that it is possible to crack what often seems to be a monolithic and invincible system of oppression.

These greats were historical firsts, and the American public has always had a great curiosity about historical firsts. Through the lens of one of these firsts, Dr. Renfroe, we can focus on a history that reveals the depth and richness of the black experience in Chicago.

First accomplishments always are difficult, because the challenger ventures into a depth of mysterious darkness never before explored. We don't know that things can be done; that dreams can be fulfilled; that great accomplishment can be realized—until somebody takes that first step, and shows the way.

Dr. Renfroe showed the way with unselfish modesty. As a pioneer, he is recognized and called attention to by his colleagues who view him, in many venues, as the ultimate role model.

Appendix: Population demographics affecting Earl Renfroe's early years

State of Illinois population figures

1810	12,282
1830	157,445
1850	851,470
1880	3,077,871
1910	5,638,591
1940	7,897,241

Of the 1940 population, 5,809,650, or 73.6 percent, lived in urban areas. Chicago alone accounted for almost three-fifths of the urban total with its population of 3,396,808.

"Whites" accounted for 95 percent of the Illinois population total in 1940; of the non-white population, practically all were considered "Negro." The non-white population of Illinois is largely concentrated in the state's cities; 92.4 percent of the 1940 non-white population lived in urban areas, with three-fourths of the urban total in the city of Chicago.

City of Chicago population figures

1920	2,701,705
1930	3,376,438
1940	3,396,808
1950	3,620,962

Around 1865, the growing industries of Illinois began to attract working-class European immigrants, particularly to Chicago, where many groups of immigrants established enclaves where they retained Old World customs and culture.

About eighty-seven percent of the population of Illinois in the decade between 1940 and 1950 was composed of American-born whites. Poles and Germans were the most numerous of the foreign-born. In 1945, there were about 400,000 blacks in the state, most of whom lived in Chicago.

More than 40 percent of the population of Illinois resides in Chicago. In 1950, out of a total Chicago population of 3,620,962, 492,265 were black.

Flying High: Earl Renfroe
Spreads His Wings

by Col. Earl Renfroe Jr.
United States Air Force (retired)

On this night in 1932, a radiant full moon over Michigan tempted the pilot of a Mercury Chic monoplane to land at an unlit, newly constructed airstrip. The sleek black craft was a modern version of a vintage World War I fighter.

The pilot was Dr. Earl Renfroe, adventurer and Captain in the Illinois National Guard. In the back seat was the legendary-to-be pilot and master mechanic Cornelius Coffey.

The Mercury Chic T-2 was a product of the best small aircraft design philosophy of the post-World War I years. It was intended as a runabout with the ability to operate out of small fields. The structure of the craft was all metal with welded steel tubing. Like today's jet fighters, it had no fixed tail surfaces. Rather, the vertical and horizontal tail surfaces were individually movable as a single piece. This made the aircraft extremely sensitive to the touch.

Even on the ground, the aircraft was a pilot's nightmare. The 28-by-4-inch high-pressure tires, lack of brakes, and a high single wing made the Mercury very difficult to handle on the ground during strong winds. Some were known to "crash" before ever becoming airborne.

Unknown to the pilot, while the runway was clear, there were substantial piles of debris adjacent to both sides of the landing strip. Earl headed toward the runway for his first night landing, reduced power, and sank into a salad bowl of darkness.

Suddenly, the pilot realized that landing at night on a dark runway presented its own special difficulties. Where exactly was the runway? The aircraft seemed to sink endlessly—then suddenly there was a wrenching contact.

In the next moments the aircraft's occupants were pinned to the right side of the cockpit as the plane spun violently to the left. The unseen piles of debris along the side of the runway had

Earl Renfroe (in cockpit) acquired his own airplane (bottom) in the 1930s.

claimed an unsuspecting victim. Finally, there was a loud crack as the propeller dug into soft earth and stalled the engine.

In a farm house nearby, Bill Baxton was relaxing after a day of farming. The unusual sound of the crash was cause for significant alarm, and a nearby plane crash was certainly enough to put your farm "on the map."

After Bill determined that Earl and his passenger were unhurt, he helped pull the aircraft onto his property for repairs. Excitement abounded as other nearby residents responded to the commotion: a real aircraft up close! And who were these daredevil pilots?

In the days that followed, the Baxton farm became the sensation of the county. The mechanics who had originally restored the Mercury Chic arrived from Chicago to effect necessary repairs. But it was when the Chic was put back in flyable condition that the real excitement would begin.

In those days, an aircraft's airworthiness needed to be approved by the Civil Aeronautics Authority. In this case, the aircraft was not located at an approved airport. This necessitated that the aircraft be flown several hundred miles to Grand Rapids, where a member of the august aeronautics body could, in fact, certify the craft's capability to fly safely.

So on a soggy morning, Earl had to attempt to take off from the area of the repair site on the Baxton farm. Since the aircraft was not equipped with an electric starter, Coffey "spun the prop." This dangerous procedure required an individual to firmly plant himself directly in front of the propeller, place both hands on one of the propeller blades and, with considerable force, whip the blade through a half circle. Many were injured or killed when balance was lost attempting such a feat.

With a successful start, Coffey climbed into the rear seat after giving the pilot a ritual slap on the back. Several of the remaining mechanics each grabbed a wing tip to turn and point the aircraft towards the widest expanse of the farm.

Earl then slowly advanced the throttle and the plane began to roll forward, progressively gathering speed. As the roll progressed across the soaked field, a flash of fear rippled through the pilot's body as he noted the trees at the field boundary. The aircraft's takeoff speed was lagging due to the wetness of the field, and it was clear that the trees were much higher than they had appeared from the takeoff position.

And so it had come—that moment in the life of an adventurer when he senses that time has slowed to a crawl, as if to emphasize the lesson being learned. As Earl looked through the rapidly spinning propeller, it appeared as if he could count each individual rotating blade. Though the aircraft had finally reached takeoff speed, it was clear that there was insufficient thrust to clear the looming treetops. Then he saw it: a slight vertical gap in the tree line—a last chance.

At the last second, with trees only inches away, Earl sharply snapped the nose of the aircraft upwards while steeply banking its wings to a near-vertical position. To the spectators across the field, the aircraft slipped through the tree effortlessly. To the pilot and passenger, Death winked ever-so weakly.

Later, at Grand Rapids, the aircraft was inspected for airworthiness and released and the crew returned to Chicago. For Earl, it marked "the experience of danger" that he seemed addicted to throughout life.

In dental school, at a time when there were no student loan programs, government grants, or scholarships to ease the burden, his job at the U.S. Post Office provided the funds for continuing education. But that Post Office work ran afoul of policies at the University of Illinois College of Dentistry that prohibited excessive part-time employment.

In fact, Earl worked the 4 p.m. to 1:30 a.m. shift at the Post Office, which constituted a full-time job. Pleading that without such employment he could not afford to remain at school, the University relented and provided a "one-time" exemption.

Since dental school courses ran from 8 a.m. to 2 p.m., Earl's effective time available for sleep averaged just three hours per night for the entirety of his dental studies. It was therefore quite remarkable that he was able to graduate ranked first in his class of 127 students. Again, it was a hunger for danger, to test the limits—and to succeed.

Shortly after graduation, Earl noticed a number of individuals repairing an aircraft in a neighborhood garage. The craft, though in a disassembled state, seemed sleek and marvelous. Though he really couldn't afford it, Earl took another chance and paid $500 for the craft—the Mercury Chic—when repairs were completed.

Fortunately, he was able to obtain an introduction to the legendary pilot and flight instructor John "The Brown Condor" Robinson, who had once been a personal pilot for Ethiopian Emperor Haile Selassie.

Before long, Earl acquired his pilot's license, which was later upgraded to "air transport commercial." To neighborhood kids, the dashing dentist became the 1932 equivalent of an astronaut.

And what of the Mercury Chic? Earl lent the craft to a fellow pilot who apparently could not cope with the sensitive nature of the controls, and consequently demolished the airplane while performing acrobatics.

While the Chic certainly qualified as a "hot" aircraft in its day, with a 90-horsepower LeBlond 7-cylinder engine capable of a daring 115 miles per hour, Earl's sense of challenge wanted more. Next, as a replacement, he acquired a bi-wing Travel Air. To fly in such an aircraft in 1934, with an astounding 225-horsepower beast of an engine, was to transcend time and space. Now Earl could travel in style, with an inertia-hand crank engine starter mechanism, a roomy cockpit, and Bendix brakes. He purchased the restored aircraft for $750 from the same group of mechanics who had repaired the Mercury Chic, and flew it for several years afterwards.

Earl's life, as well as those of millions of others, was abruptly changed by the eruption of the Second World War. Predictably, the danger-seeker volunteered for the Army Air Corps. Despite his impressive flight credentials, his age—over 30 and therefore too old—disqualified him from flight duty. Though he investigated every route, both political and personal, Earl was unable to obtain a waiver to the pilot age limit. On the other hand, his dental specialty and his being a commissioned officer in the National Guard guaranteed that he would con-

Major Renfroe took command of and reorganized the dental corps at Fort Huachuca, Arizona, during World War II.

tribute to the war effort.

Called to active duty in the National Guard, Earl was posted to the 184th Field Artillery Division at Fort Custer, Michigan. Here, his duties consisted primarily of training cadres (trained personnel capable of taking control and, in turn, training others) for other dental units. He quickly was promoted to Major and transferred to Fort Gordon, Georgia, which unfortunately was a "dead-end" assignment and inappropriate for an officer of his rank. Incensed, he posted a furious letter to Army headquarters expressing his indignation. HQ agreed, and sent Major Renfroe to Fort Huachuca, Arizona, next to the famous town of Tombstone and home of the 92nd Infantry Division.

This outfit was undergoing training for combat in Italy, and Major Renfroe's arrival upset the apple cart. It seems that the resident—and incompetent—Dental Unit commander was grooming a close friend to succeed him, but Major Renfroe outranked the understudy. This resulted in Major Renfroe being shuffled around to various "learning" duties to prevent his assuming full authoritative command.

Curiously, Army HQ had not forgotten about this unusual major and followed his assignment with a letter directing that he be given duties appropriate to his rank and experience. This high-level intervention had immediate ramifications. The Dental Unit commander was shuffled "upstairs" to duties for which his incompetence would be less obvious. This action, which elevated Major Renfroe to the position of Commander, would shake up the status quo.

For at Fort Huachuca, there were two kinds of dental officers: those who were functional to the 92nd Division, and cadre dentists, who remained at the fort regardless of the disposition of the 92nd. The cadre dentists were forced to carry the load of patients, while the good old boys of the 92nd perfected their combat skills—on the golf course.

Upon assuming command, Major Renfroe called all dental officers together to redefine their duties.

Henceforth, all fort dentists would be present for duty during the duty day, and cadre dentists would henceforth assume no greater patient load than 92nd personnel. Within weeks of this change of policy, an HQ major with a dental background was assigned to the fort in "casual" status—ostensibly meaning awaiting assignment and not injected into the unit chain-of-command.

The mystery major was apparently sent to observe the deportment of the dental unit under Major Renfroe, to determine if he was some sort of loose cannon, perhaps brilliant but lacking in leadership skills. After a month of observation, however, HQ's major was satisfied that Major Renfroe was simply a hard task-master who was fair to his subordinates. Before departing, the evaluator remarked to Major Renfroe that he was "doing a good job."

But Major Renfroe was yet to experience his greatest personal challenge at Fort Huachuca. This arose over the denial of prestige housing quarters for cadre dental officers. When the 92nd

Division shipped out for combat duty in Italy, the vacant top-of-the-line quarters should have been made available for cadre dental officers of appropriate rank. In particular, Major Renfroe felt that his family deserved the large, single-family home on "Officers Row," a lovely area set upon a steep incline overlooking the fort.

Major Renfroe could determine no logical reason why he and other cadre officers should be kept in poor, second-class quarters instead of the better housing that was both unoccupied and available. With Major Renfroe having exhausted all formal chain-of-command avenues of redress, Commanding General Kent offered a court of last resort.

Admitted to the general's office, Major Renfroe carefully and precisely enunciated his "right" to occupy a better class of living quarters. After all, he was the next-in-line ranking officer. The general was impassive and non-responsive until the major, known to be rather "uppity," suggested the magic inference. Was there "some other" reason he was being denied the quarters?

Immediately, General Kent went ballistic. Was Major Renfroe bringing up the unmentionable, the unthinkable—the "race thing?" The major feigned surprise and stated that there was no logical reason he could think of for denial of the quarters; did the general have the missing explanation? Predictably, the audience ended rather abruptly with the major intending to dust off the old typewriter for another letter to HQ.

But suddenly, before a letter could be drafted, the long sought-after quarters suddenly became available. The new residence suited Major and Mrs. Renfroe perfectly and served as a comfortable haven until the end of World War II.

Earl and Hilda then returned to Chicago along with thousands of other GIs to re-establish themselves in a society they had been away from for four years. Times were difficult as society readjusted to a peacetime economy, and Dr. Renfroe's dental income wasn't enough. So he found himself, once again, working at the Post Office.

In an attempt to escape the limited economic confines of his neighborhood clientele, Dr. Renfroe sought to establish his dental practice in downtown Chicago's "Loop." Unfortunately, nothing appropriate seemed to be available. For while there were plenty of vacant offices listed for rent, they all suddenly seemed to be "on hold" when Earl showed up.

Dr. Renfroe particularly wanted a certain Dearborn Street office, which he had determined would suit his practice best. The building manager seemed to have one excuse after another why the vacant office couldn't be leased. Happily, Dr. Renfroe's encounter with the building's owner revealed that the delaying tactics were entirely the doing of the building manager. Indignant, the owner instructed that Dr. Renfroe be leased the facility of his choice.

So once again, it had been Dr. Renfroe against the world. No organization or body of laws supported him, and no news story to engender the support of a civil rights group would be written. He literally was on his own. Racism had been defeated in Germany, but it was alive and well in Chicago.

He even took some heat from his own friends, as many advised him not to move out of a neighborhood where he had established a fine reputation and not to quit general dentistry for orthodontics, which many felt would not be economically viable. But their concerns turned out to be groundless and the decision proved appropriate.

A new patient, "Buckteeth Bill," had teeth that were slanted so far forward that his lips were unable to close. He came to the orthodontic chair of Dr. Renfroe with a bundle of personality problems and a massive inferiority complex. Over a period of time, the metal bands looped around his teeth slowly pulled them back into the mouth, to the benefit of both the dental and mental health of the patient.

Many of Dr. Renfroe's patients were minorities whose finances were stretched to the breaking point by this specialized form of dentistry. But after two years of wearing braces, the patients often underwent a dramatic change of personality that was well-worth the monetary cost. Dr. Renfroe remembers that many patients, after treatment, suddenly married. The confi-

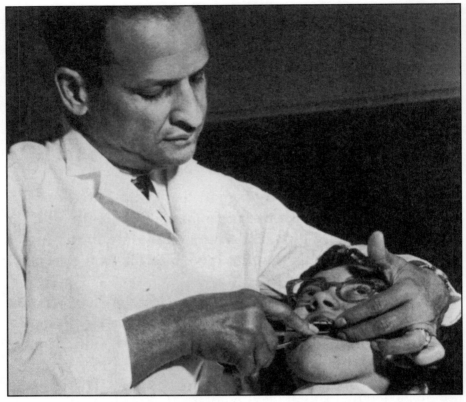

Dr. Earl Renfroe, the first black orthodontist to have an office in Chicago's Loop.

dence engendered by their new appearance let them get on with normal lives.

In time, though Dr. Renfroe's downtown practice began to flourish, he couldn't resist additional challenges. He thus set his sights on competing for the post of head of the Department of Orthodontics at the UIC College of Dentistry.

Initially, Dr. Renfroe was placed in charge of the department's division responsible for "technical-mechanical production," a "blue-collar" unit not populated by the department's rising stars, who gravitated to the research division and had an inside track for promotions. The situation was an embarrassment to all since most of the dental researchers were former students of Dr. Renfroe's.

However, since cream really does rise to the top, Dr. Renfroe methodically assumed an ascending chain of positions culminating in head of the department. But this was not to be the end of remarkable attainments for him.

On the strength of recommendations by Brazilian students who had attended the UIC College of Dentistry, Dr. Renfroe was invited to attend a convention of the São Paulo State Orthodontic Society. Although slated to give the keynote address, Dr. Renfroe spoke no Portuguese.

Not satisfied with having his remarks translated at the convention, Dr. Renfroe decided to attend the Berlitz Institute and learn the language. Needless to say, he was a smash hit and was eternally endeared to those professionals attending.

For many years thereafter, Dr. Renfroe was frequently requested to return to assist Brazilian universities and dental professionals. His acclaimed book *Technique Training in Orthodonics* became an instructional guide for the Brazilian army. Finally, he was offered the position of head of orthodontics for Riberato Preto in São Paulo, which he declined.

Senior academic offerings were routine for Dr. Renfroe. Another appointment offer he turned down was that of head of the Department of Graduate Orthodontics at the College of Physicians and Surgeons in San Francisco.

Dr. Renfroe's background left him with a strong distaste for the hopelessness expressed by some—especially those who feel that government assistance or some form of umbrella or civic group is necessary for personal advancement. He was clear that while his opinion in no way denigrated advances, both individual and collective, that have been achieved in recent years, he felt strongly that the individual must never feel that his or her path is somehow blocked unless some type of outside assistance is available. One's role model should be the individual who achieves recognition because of, not in spite of, personal credentials.

Dr. Renfroe had a simple credo: Don't accept the system's rules blindly and, by all means, challenge the system if it hinders your ability to achieve greatness.

Into his 90s, he still expressed strong opinions. He was quick to offer his thoughts on the modern dentist being seated while the patient reclines. This "advance," to Dr. Renfroe's way of thinking, did not in and of itself facilitate better dentistry. Rather, he saw it as a convenience that promotes higher patient production—a "commercial idea" he considered somewhat "strange." Another development along those lines is the reliance of modern dentists on mostly preconstructed or manufactured devices and aids all designed to expedite greater patient flow per unit of time. Previously, Dr. Renfroe recalled, dentists consumed a great deal of time custom-constructing individual devices for the patient's mouth.

In Dr. Renfroe's opinion, his connection with Brazilian dentistry ranked as the most fulfilling of his professional career. Initially, Brazilian dentistry was several decades behind urban United States state-of-the-art. Essentially, this was due to excessive tooth extraction, which Brazilian dentists performed rather than solving tooth and gum problems through preventive dentistry. Today, Brazilian dentistry is on a par with the best that can be seen in North America, and Brazil sets the standard for all of South America.

Dr. Renfroe set the standard on the fabrication of orthodontic band and malocclusion analysis with his signal literary work, *Edgewise*, focusing on formalized treatment plans. The book also has been translated into Japanese.

His achievements are a matter of record in past editions of *Who's Who in America* and *Who's Who in the World*. He is featured in an exhibit on American blacks in aviation, "Black Wings," at the Smithsonian Institution's National Air and Space Museum in Washington, DC. In 80 years of civic involvement, Dr. Renfroe held membership in countless organizations, among them the National Conference of Christians and Jews, the Chicago Urban League, and the Chicago Council on Foreign Relations, which he served as vice president.

A successful family man, my father Earl Renfroe reared me, a retired United States Air Force Colonel and pilot; and he and his wife of more than a half century, Hilda, had two children— Diane, a partner in the Arthur Andersen accounting firm, and

Stephen, who recently retired from the Air Force as an air traffic controller.

It can truly be said that in whatever endeavor he tried, Earl Renfroe spread his wings and was successful. What a life!

Dr. Earl Renfroe's Impact on Orthodontics in Brazil

by Paulo Affonso de Freitas, DDS

Although orthodontics is the oldest specialty in dentistry, in the 1950s in Brazil, as in much of the rest of the world outside of Europe and the United States, its development was only beginning. Before that time, there were few professionals working in this field, and patients often did not even know they needed treatment. For that matter, most of them were not aware that the science of orthodontics existed.

Brazilian dentists who wanted to improve their knowledge had to go abroad, either to the United States or to Europe. At the time, there was the general impression that Americans favored fixed appliances, while Europeans tended to use removable appliances.

To those interested in orthodontics, Dr. Allan G. Brodie Sr. was well-known, and the Department of Orthodontics he chaired at UIC was considered to be one of the best in the world. For this reason, Brazilian dentists seeking orthodontic training started coming to Chicago for their graduate studies. Once there, they learned that Dr. Brodie was not alone in the ranks of gifted faculty members in that department.

Among them, Dr. Earl W. Renfroe was one of the shiniest stars, possessing deep scientific knowledge and remarkable skill with his hands. His Brazilian students saw that with this profile, Dr. Renfroe was the ideal professional to come to Brazil and teach their colleagues the art and science of Edward Angle (1855-1930), who is considered the "father" of orthodontics.

The first Brazilian to graduate from the UIC College of Dentistry's Department of Orthodontics was Dr. Alvaro Rubem Marcondes, who received his master's degree in 1956 after two fruitful years under the guidance of Drs. Brodie and Renfroe. Dr. Marcondes was most impressed with the high quality of the program.

For this reason, in 1959, three years after Dr. Marcondes'

Dr. Renfroe (3rd from left) with Brazilian colleagues at the Congresso Odontologico Riograndense. Stephen Renfroe, Dr. Renfroe's youngest son, is at right.

return to Brazil, through his influence the São Paulo State Orthodontic Society invited Dr. Renfroe to conduct a practical course with emphasis on the edgewise technique. Although Dr. Renfroe did not speak Portuguese, he felt the responsibility to learn the language specifically so he could teach the course.

Approximately 20 professionals from different regions of the country attended, including this writer, and we are able to confirm Dr. Marcondes' favorable impression about Dr. Renfroe's ability. The course was a great success, and Dr. Renfroe returned to teach in Brazil again in 1960.

That year the second Brazilian to be trained under Drs. Brodie and Renfroe at UIC, Dr. Carlos Jorge Vogel, graduated with his master's degree. Upon his return to Brazil, he conveyed the same excellent impressions about his graduate work and about Dr. Renfroe.

Dr. Renfroe came back to Brazil in 1963 under the invitation of Dr. Manoel Carlos Muller de Araújo, head of the Department of Orthodontics in Piracicaba, SP, where Dr. Renfroe was a guest speaker and taught a short course during a national orthodontic meeting. While Dr. Renfroe was in Brazil, the dean of the dental school at Ribierao Preto, SP, offered Dr. Renfroe the opportunity to become department head of orthodontics there, which unfortunately for orthodontics in Brazil he decided to decline. A year later, the Brazilian Army made Dr. Renfroe's *Technique Training in Orthodontics* a requirement for its dentists.

In the years that followed, six other Brazilian professionals attended graduate courses in orthodontics at UIC, most of them earning master's degrees: Drs. Oscar de Alencar Aquino (1964), João Ramos de Freitas (1968), Roberto Antonio Trevisan (1973), Anna Leticia C.C. Lima and Roberto M.A. Lima Filho (1975), and Joaõ Carlos Cerqueira Dias (1976).

In the 1960s and 1970s, Dr. Renfroe was published consistently in Brazilian dental journals, and his book *Edgewise* became a best-seller among Brazilian orthodontists. In those decades

Dr. Renfroe (far left) listens to a translation at a 1976 orthodontics congress in São Paulo. The earphones were just a formality, however, as he had learned Portuguese in 1959 specifically to teach in Brazil.

and after he returned many times to Brazil, teaching in Rio de Janeiro, Porto Alegre, and other places. His Brazilian experiences also gave him the opportunity to teach elsewhere in South America, including Argentina and Peru.

Dr. Renfroe continues to be well-remembered by his Brazilian students. Dr. Oscar de Alencar Aquino says, "To talk about Dr. Renfroe is, at the same time, an easy and a very difficult mission. It is easy to look at him with detachment as a prominent professional recognized all over the world. In ministering classes at the UIC College of Dentistry or developing seminars in Brazil, through his skill he oriented and capacitized many professionals.

"On the other hand, it is very difficult to talk about Dr. Renfroe as a man without addressing the aspects of his personality deeply devoted to the human being. His respect for people carries him to easy and friendly relationships; to a didactic comprehension of the rhythm and individuality of each person; to a placement of a right word in the right moment to the person who needs it; and, overall, to a special way of teaching and evaluating. The words 'dignity,' 'respect' for people, and 'competence' define Dr. Renfroe as a man and a specialist in orthodontics," he concluded.

At the dawn of the third millennium, it has been many years since Dr. Renfroe's first visit to Brazil—but he still is remembered with fond memories by all those who had the opportunity to meet him and his lovely wife, Hilda, and who benefited from his knowledge and kindness. He will always be remembered as an outstanding educator, and a good friend.

I had the privilege of being a colleague and close friend of Dr. Renfroe's for 40 years. I can testify unequivocally that Dr. Renfroe had a highly positive impact. Since he began teaching Brazilian professionals, both at UIC and in their homeland itself, orthodontics in Brazil has never been the same.

The Renfroe-Barbados Connection
by Ronald A. Ramsay, BDS, Cert. Orth.

Professor Earl W. Renfroe established his initial connection with Barbados when he met and married the stunning Hilda Forte, who is Barbadian by parentage and birth, on December 24, 1942. Her family and mine have been close friends for three generations. The Renfroe family later fell into the agreeable habit of vacationing in Barbados on a regular basis. "The water's always warm and the weather's never bad," Dr. Renfroe said.

This writer first was introduced to Dr. Renfroe around 1960, when I was just 15 and mainly attracted to his beautiful daughter, Diane. I soon became dimly aware of Dr. Renfroe's growing prestige in the world of dental academe, and was even privileged to see the manuscript for his textbook *Edgewise* before it was published—although at the time it meant little to me. That would change.

At Christmas 1969, upon my return to Barbados immediately following my final examination in dentistry at the University of Bristol, England, I told Dr. Renfroe of my new-found interest in orthodontics and my intention to pursue that specialty in the United Kingdom. Much to my dismay, he strongly advised me instead to set my sights on the United States. I nevertheless returned to England where, after a year of internship, I recognized the wisdom of Dr. Renfroe's advice and returned once more to Barbados, to work and to save while applying for admission to orthodontic programs in the U.S.

Dr. J. Daniel Subtelny, chair of the Department of Orthodontics at the Eastman Dental Center in Rochester, NY, accepted my application in 1975. Dr. Subtelny, a 1953 graduate of the UIC College of Dentistry orthodontics program, had studied under the legendary Drs. Allan G. Brodie Sr. and Earl W. Renfroe, and often spoke in glowing terms of Dr. Renfroe's mastery and expertise.

Upon graduation from the Eastman Dental Center I returned to Barbados to the remnant of my general dentistry practice and hung out my orthodontic shingle. Dr. Renfroe's confidence in

(Left to right) Dr. Ronald A. Ramsay; his wife, Marlene; Hilda Renfroe; and Dr. Earl Renfroe at the Renfroe Professional Centre in Barbados.

the quality of the training I had received at Eastman, his faith in my ability to succeed, and his acting as an advisor during the early years of my practice provided from the start a much-needed boost, so that before long I was able not only to construct a customized office building, which I named the Renfroe Professional Centre to recognize his contribution to the development of orthodontics, but also to limit my practice exclusively to orthodontics both in Barbados and in neighboring Trinidad.

Dr. Renfroe officially opened the facility in December of 1980, and at each subsequent visit to Barbados, even though he was supposedly retired, he would spend a considerable amount of time in the office discussing cases, providing valuable insights from his vast experience, and encouraging me to treat the seemingly untreatable. One such memorable case of a daunting bilateral buccal cross-bite, or "Brodie Syndrome," over which I had procrastinated for a year, was successfully treated only after Dr.

Renfroe retrieved the records of a similar case from his extensive archives at UIC and mailed copies to me in order to strengthen my clinical courage.

Much as my patients and I appreciated and benefited from Dr. Renfroe's frequent visits to the growing practice that proudly bears his name, the aspect of his character I most came to admire was his genuine humility and quiet magnanimity, especially in regard to the ethnic discrimination above which he had so constantly towered.

On a personal note, my wife, Marlene, and I were immensely grateful when, at one hour's notice, Dr. Renfroe relieved me at chairside so that I could be present at bedside for the birth of our daughter, Natasha Lynn, on the morning of January 13, 1979.

In January 1997, after a ten-year lapse, we were honored once again by Dr. Renfroe's presence in Barbados. This time it was for the celebration, with his wife, children, and grandchildren, of his 90th birthday. On that occasion he delivered a memorable speech at the Renfroe Professional Centre, where he was honored with a plaque recognizing with gratitude and admiration the long and illustrious career of this gentle giant, his invaluable pioneering influence both in the world of orthodontics and in our little island-world of Barbados.

Over the years, our love and respect for Earl have grown and grown, so that in this corner of the world, we will be eternally indebted to him for his shining example as one of life's rare heroes.

Teacher and Colleague

by William S. Bike and Mark J. Valentino
University of Illinios at Chicago College of Dentistry
Office of Advancement and Alumni Affairs

Dr. Cyril Sadowsky, who earned his MS in orthodontics from the UIC College of Dentistry in 1971, and Dr. Bernard Schneider, a graduate of both the College's DDS (1954) and MS in orthodontics (1956) programs, first met Dr. Earl Renfroe during their student days.

They then went on to distinguished teaching careers of their own in the College's Department of Orthodontics. Dr. Sadowsky is a professor, and Dr. Schneider is a retired clinical professor. The duo is so well-respected that recently, College alumni and colleagues established the Schnieder/Sadowsky Faculty Fund, which will provide financial support for faculty-sponsored research and other needs.

Both, therefore, are highly qualified to rate Dr. Renfroe as teacher and colleague—and friend.

"Even as a student, I felt he was a very disciplined individual," Dr. Sadowsky recalled. "He had excellent hands, and was a wonderful teacher."

Dr. Sadowsky's student era is renowned as one in which faculty were particularly—some say excessively—tough on students. But with Dr. Renfroe, "there wasn't a feeling of intimidation," Dr. Sadowsky said. "Oh, everyone knew what he expected of them—excellence and your best efforts. But it was very refreshing to me to be in the environment he created in which you could really enjoy what you were doing."

Dr. Schneider agrees. "Dr. Renfroe was admired and respected by our students," he said. "Whoever he taught has good memories of him because he didn't have agendas. He was just a good guy."

Remembering his freshman impression of Dr. Renfroe, Dr. Schneider recalled, "He was a very articulate, suave, professional person whom I thought had wonderful skills—even in tooth carving. He had great manual dexterity—to watch him work

"He had excellent hands, and was a wonderful teacher," Dr. Sadowsky recalled.

with his hands was special. I thought Dr. Renfroe was a gifted orthodontist, a gifted teacher. He did beautiful work."

"His technical ability to really bend and manipulate orthodontic wires was excellent," Dr. Sadowsky recalled. "He wrote the book on technique—literally—and he influenced people for at least 30 years in the orthodontic technical point of view."

"He was very careful with what he said and how he said it— Dr. Renfroe conducted himself with a certain elegance," Dr. Schneider explained. "He was highly skilled and really taught me how to treat cases. I mean, it was just a pleasure to watch him do anything. Everyone felt that way—his cases in the clinic were not only well-attended, they were under control and turned out well."

In Dr. Schneider's era, two giants in the orthodontics field, Drs. Renfroe and Dr. Allan G. Brodie Sr., ran the College's orthodontic program. "Dr. Brodie's expertise was in didactics," Dr. Schneider said, "whereas Dr. Renfroe's was in diagnosis, treatment planning, and clinical management."

Dr. Schneider joined the faculty in 1957, and blossomed after Dr. Renfroe took over from Dr. Brodie in chairing the orthodontics department in 1966. "Dr. Renfroe just kept promoting me, which I hardly even asked for," Dr. Schneider recalled. "He made it his business to move me along and really encouraged me to stay with teaching."

Even during Dr. Renfroe's short retirement in the early 1970s, as a good judge of teaching talent he was instrumental in accelerating Dr. Sadowsky's career on the faculty—and improving his lot in life—as well. A South African national, Dr. Sadowsky had, since his graduation "been communicating with Dr. Renfroe from back in South Africa, and through him I learned that there was going to be a new department head in orthodontics, Dr. John F. Cleall, who was looking for full-time faculty," Dr.

Two giants in the orthodontics field, Dr. Allan G. Brodie Sr. (left) and Dr. Renfroe, colleagues in the UIC College of Dentistry's orthodontic program.

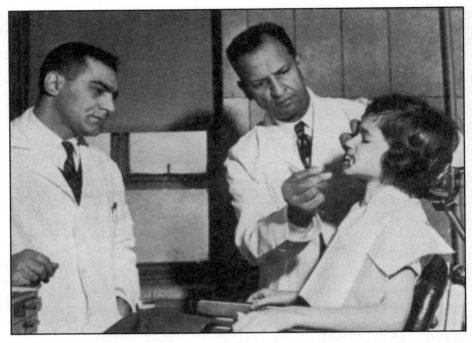

"Dr. Renfroe was extremely inventive and creative in how he treated cases, so often he didn't have to take teeth out...," Dr. Schneider said.

Sadowsky said.

"As a student I had been impressed with both the academic environment and the openness of society in the United States," Dr. Sadowsky continued. His family "always wanted to immigrate, but it isn't easy. Then Dr. Renfroe put me in touch with the new department head, and that's what allowed us to immigrate here in 1976."

It was not unusual for Dr. Renfroe to have a positive impact on students' and colleagues' families. "My father and mother visited here just before I started the program and they were really impressed and had a wonderful interaction with Dr. Renfroe," Dr. Sadowsky recalled. "The warmth that my dad felt for him continues to this very day. He was always saying to be sure to give Dr. Renfroe his best wishes, and he hadn't seen him for 25 years."

Perhaps Dr. Renfroe considered the importance of the family's influence on career because it was a family member who got him to go into dentistry in the first place. "It just seemed that every time my mother would talk to me, she had dentistry on her mind," Dr. Renfroe recalled. "I never had to worry about what I was going to be. I was the one to be the dentist. I had nothing to do with it—she did it all herself," he chuckled.

Dr. Schneider was pleased to have been on hand for the passing of the mantle of chair of the orthodontics department from one giant, Dr. Brodie, to another, Dr. Renfroe.

"The two had different management styles," Dr. Schneider recalled. "Dr. Brodie was a little more autocratic. Although Dr. Brodie, once you got to know him, was wonderful and would spend time with you, there was a certain distance. That wasn't there with Dr. Renfroe, whom you always felt was more approachable."

There were differences in treatment philosophy as well. "Dr. Brodie was very much non-extraction in his treatment philosophy," Dr. Schneider said. "Dr. Renfroe was far less that way, but Dr. Renfroe was extremely inventive and creative in how he treated cases, so often he didn't have to take teeth out anyway. But he was perfectly willing to say, 'there are cases in which we've got to take out teeth and when we do, this is how.' I agree that you've got to take out teeth in certain cases—the key is which ones. The right decision is what makes the good practitioner stand out."

Both Drs. Brodie and Renfroe are considered to be orthodontic pioneers, but Dr. Brodie seems to have achieved the more widespread reputation, although orthodontists in Brazil, where Dr. Renfroe is considered a "father" of the discipline, may disagree.

"Dr. Brodie always seemed to be a major speaker of the American Association of Orthodontists and at orthodontic meetings," Dr. Schneider said. "They both wrote articles, but Dr. Brodie wrote more than 100. Dr. Renfroe was well-respected, but you had to spend time with him to truly appreciate his gifts."

Such speeches and articles often focused on the theoretical; the practical often is just less glamorous. "Dr. Brodie was quite good—he was a theoretical man," Dr. Renfroe once said. "I was a practical man interested in mechanics, so we worked quite well together."

Dr. Renfroe retired from the College in 1973, but couldn't stay away, coming back as a volunteer during the 1980s. Drs. Schneider and Sadowsky then had the pleasure of working alongside Dr. Renfroe once again. "He was in such great physical shape he almost danced around," Dr. Sadowsky recalled. "He was an elderly man and here he was, still doing his thing."

"He would come around and counsel us," Dr. Schneider said. "He was still extremely supportive of the department and extremely giving in every way."

"It would be really fun calling on him for a historical perspective that brought a richness to our seminars," Dr. Sadowsky noted.

With faculty like Drs. Sadowsky, Schneider, Brodie, and of course, Renfroe, UIC's Department of Orthodontics' influence has been second to none. "I think we gave birth to a dozen department heads, and they spread out and spread their message," Dr. Schnieder said. "The whole profession was elevated. I'm not sure if you'll ever find another department that will dominate the way we did. Dr. Renfroe was one of the major reasons why."

The Best Mirror

by William S. Bike
Associate Director of Advancement and Alumni Affairs
University of Illinois at Chicago College of Dentistry

"The best mirror is an old friend," wrote the 17th Century English poet George Herbert. Drs. Sadowsky and Schneider are only two of the many of students and colleagues who have become Dr. Earl Renfroe's friends, in whom he can see the reflection of a life well lived.

"I've had letters from so many students thanking me," Dr. Renfroe recalled. "It made me feel quite good."

The following are a few telling excerpts of letters sent to Dr. Renfroe, and comments made about him, from friends.

"Your clinical and administrative experience and judgment is a talent rarely encountered in professional education....Orthodontics at the University of Illinois has enjoyed an enviable reputation throughout the world. To a large extent, Earl, the clinical excellence of its graduates is the result of your instruction and guidance."

—John J. Byrne, DDS

"...thank you for helping make it possible for me to pursue a lifetime of happiness in orthodontics."

—Gerald H. Borden, DDS

"I have thought of you often and the tremendous positive impact you had upon my life as my teacher and friend. Rarely has an opportunity escaped me, especially during my teaching experiences, that I fail to mention your name and give you credit for anything good that I might have accomplished in my orthodontic career. Your meticulous attention to detail and thorough knowledge of the basic principles of orthodontics that you taught us guided me through many treacherous pathways."

—Edward Hamilton, DDS

51

"I am very proud to have had you as my teacher."
—Art Gauss, DDS

"You have always been an inspiration for me, and I am very grateful for your guidance."
—David B. Olson, DDS

"I join the City of Chicago in commending you for the positive and lasting impact your lifelong hard work and giving has had on future generations and institutions in Chicago."
—U.S. Senator Alan Dixon

"I had always considered you the finest teacher I ever had and felt whatever caliber of clinical orthodontist graduated...was entirely due to your patience and skill in getting your concepts across to us."
—Stanley Rosenthal, DDS

"As a teacher, you have few equals...."
—Allan G. Brodie Jr., DDS

"When you are taught to think basic concepts, as you have taught all your students, you should be able to separate the good from the bad. I feel that this is what you gave me and I will always be indebted to you....one of the best damn orthodontic teachers in the world."
—R.J. Herberger, DDS

"I am proud to know him, and to have had him as one of my teachers and colleagues. I can attest to his passion for teaching and to his commitment to any student who came to him for guidance. "
—Allen W. Anderson, DDS, MS
Dean, UIC College of Dentistry, 1987-99

"The orthodontic program at Illinois was great for two reasons: Drs. Bill Downs and Earl Renfroe. Bill and Earl had the "right stuff." While serving as chair of orthodontics at Loma Linda in the '60s, I had Earl as a continuing education lecturer and demonstrator. He had the skill and discipline to train his students to a keen clinical edge. I

number Earl among my finest colleagues."

—Thomas J. Zwember, DDS

"We respected him as an authority on the edgewise appliance. He knew more about the edgewise system's versatiltity and application than anybody else. I think of him as 'the edgewise spirit.' He was so enthusiastic about developments in the field. His book on the edgewise applicance truly is a historical document. It is an excellent review of othodontics in that generation.

"His hand-eye motor proclivity was extraordinary. Said Brodie of Renfroe, 'You ought to see that guy park a car.' Everything was done with absolute precision and control.

"I enjoyed his sense of humor. When he laughed, he laughed all over."

—Robert M. Ricketts, DDS

In 2000, Dr. Daniel J. Pyevich, a 1974 graduate of the orthodontics program, sent an unsolicited testimonial to the College's alumni magazine praising Dr. Renfroe. The Renfroe family was so moved by Dr. Pyevich's words that they asked Dr. Zane F. Muhl, the UIC College of Dentistry's interim associate dean for academic affairs and a graduate of the orthodontics program, to read excerpts at the memorial service the College held for Dr. Renfroe on Dec. 16, 2000.

Dr. Pyevich wrote that Dr. Renfroe "had a profound effect" on students, pointing out that he was an "inspirational teacher and mentor to hundreds."

He went on to say that "It is the qualities of dignity and professionalism that most impressed me upon my first contact with Dr. Renfroe," for Dr. Renfroe addressed Dr. Pyevich and his classmates "not as lowly freshmen...but as if we were distinguished members of some national orthodontic society...Our appreciation only grew each week."

Dr. Pyevich noted that "Dr. Renfroe's impression on me left little doubt that this not only was the area of dentistry for me, but that his program was where I wanted to study orthodontics....he displayed many additional qualities during the next 21 months that made him what I feel is truly a giant in the field of orthodontic education."

Dr. Pyevich was impressed that although Dr. Renfroe was writing a book and running a busy practice, "He spent much time in the seminar room with each class discussing clinical cases and mechanics, and he personally supervised cases in the clinic with each student." And, Dr. Pyevich noted, Dr. Renfroe's office was always open, "so one could walk right in whenever one wished to see him.

"It is a testimony to the man," Dr. Pyevich continued, "that despite all the injustices and indignities to which he was subjected...Dr. Renfroe could carry himself throughout his career in the distinguished and admirable fashion...which marks the heights of professionalism.

"Hundreds of highly competent and successful orthodontists throughout the country are thankful for this," Dr. Pyevich concluded.

Dr. Muhl said he agreed with Dr. Pyevich's sentiments, "with one slight amendment. Orthodontists all over the world, not just in the United States, are better because they studied with Dr. Earl Renfroe. If a legacy of a gifted teacher is superb students who go on to achieve their own greatness, then Dr. Renfroe has indeed left the world a wonderful legacy," Dr. Muhl concluded.

The last word, as always, is that of Dr. Renfroe, who in his 90s commented on teaching. "I wouldn't mind being out there every day again," said Dr. Renfroe. "I just loved to do my work."

Textbooks by the 'Practical Man'

by William S. Bike
Associate Director of Advancement and Alumni Affairs
University of Illinois at Chicago College of Dentistry

"I was a practical man interested in mechanics," Dr. Earl W. Renfroe said as he recalled his days teaching orthodontics. When this practical man saw a need for orthodontic textbooks on mechanics, he came up with a practical solution—he wrote them himself.

"Many of the technical aspects of orthodontics traditionally had to have been learned from directly observing somebody doing them, often several times, because they were not written down," said Dr. Carla Evans, professor and head of the Department of Orthodontics at the UIC College of Dentistry. "Dr. Renfroe took the time to write them down and make them available to people."

His first book, *Technique Training in Orthodontics*, was published by Edwards Brothers Inc. of Ann Arbor, MI, in 1960. It was a definite improvement over the observation/repetition method mentioned by Dr. Evans. As the world-renowned Dr. Allan G. Brodie, chair of the UIC College of Dentistry Department of Orthodontics at the time, wrote in the book's forward, "There is a rather general tendency to believe that the mere repetition of an act, over and over again, will ultimately lead to improved performance. This is far from true. The only individual who benefits from practicing is the one who puts mental effort into the practice... [who] seeks to find the reason behind each point of success or failure."

Technique Training provided some of those reasons and encouraged that mental effort, in an attempt to make orthodontists "far less apt to waste time repeating the same error," Dr. Brodie wrote. "Such thoughtful practice has other rewards that are not so easily understood. These involve the little-understood relationships between neuromuscular control and self-confidence. As confidence increases, coordination improves and vice versa. The operator who has not mastered a given technique

55

Decades of orthodontic expertise proved invaluable when Dr. Renfroe wrote his two textbooks.

approaches it with misgivings and shaky hands, or which is worse, avoids it entirely and substitutes for it an inferior procedure of less difficulty."

Dr. Brodie called excellent technical performance "the most valuable hand-maiden to successful practice." He wrote that "Dr. Renfroe has demonstrated thoroughly his ability to handle the technical demands of all appliances," and that *Technique Training* "bears mute testimony to his meticulous attention to the smallest details." The execution of the illustrations, "most of them by his own hands, reveals the deep thought that has gone into the preparation of this book," Dr. Brodie wrote.

Described by Dr. Brodie as "a great aid to the beginner in orthodontics," the book also was written by Dr. Renfroe as a help to the orthodontist "who finds himself in a maze of 'improvements,' gadgets, and philosophies...," Dr. Renfroe wrote. At the time, there were more than 15 designs of edgewise brackets on the market, and *Technique Training* proved a welcome guidebook through that maze of manufacturers' claims.

"All without advertisement," Dr. Renfroe wrote a few years later, "it had several printings to meet the demands of individuals and schools in the United States and Canada." The book became well-known in Brazil, where Dr. Renfroe described the demand as "insatiable," and also enjoyed popularity in Western Europe, since specialists there favored the fixed appliances in orthodontic treatment that *Technique Training* described so well.

So vital was this publication that the Brazilian Army made it required reading for its dentists beginning in 1964.

By the 1970s, those previous works had exhausted themselves, according to Dr. Renfroe, so he wrote a new book, *Edgewise.* Published by Lea & Febiger of Philadelphia in 1975,

"I know the students still pick up the books [written by Dr. Renfroe] and read them and find the information worthwhile," said Dr. Carla Evans. Above, two UIC College of Dentistry orthodontics students examine Edgewise *early in 1999.*

the book was devoted exclusively to the edgewise appliance, providing the reader with "virtually everything he needs to know about its use, design, construction, modifications, and historical background," according to the publisher.

Organized into two sections, the book includes information about orthodontic techniques, instruments, and materials in part one, and philosophies of diagnosis, treatment planning, and case studies in part two. An additional improvement over the illustrations in *Technique Training* was the inclusion of photographs in *Edgewise*. The latter book was a successful attempt "to meet the many innovations in appliance construction and treatment" since the publication of *Technique Training*, according to Dr. Renfroe.

Again, Dr. Renfroe wrote his book to "stimulate thinking," for "the appliance is only as good as" the orthodontist "who assembles and uses it," according to Dr. Renfroe. He designed *Edgewise* "to stimulate logical thinking and the application of logic to simple, efficient appliance construction in the treatment of malocclusion," he wrote.

Once again, Dr. Renfroe had penned a book that proved an international success. In fact, there was such interest in *Edgewise* abroad that only two years later, a Japanese firm, Shorin, decided to publish the book in the Far East.

A quarter-century later, Dr. Renfroe's textbooks have been overtaken by time—but not completely. "They were comprehensive and very detailed explanations of orthodontic appliances and their versatility," Dr. Evans explained. "As opposed to diagnostic information, since technical information changes with time, many of the things described in those books have been replaced with newer versions. Direct bonding made things very different in orthodontics.

"But a person wanting to use a fixed appliance would still find things they could use in this book," Dr. Evans noted. "I know the students still pick up the books and read them and find the information worthwhile."

Although now out-of-print, *Edgewise* still can be obtained through internet booksellers Amazon.com, Barnesandnoble.com, and Borders.com. It also is available as a paperbound book or on microfilm from UMI of Ann Arbor, MI, through its Books on Demand program. Through the program, UMI will create copies of an out-of-print classic such as *Edgewise* for an interested purchaser.

"I think the greatness of the writing lies in the superb level of detail and precision with which it was put together," Dr. Evans concluded.

Dr. Renfroe was the perfect author for the texts, because of his unique mechanical ability. According to Dr. Andrew J. Haas, a 1958 graduate of the orthodontics program at the UIC College of Dentistry, "In my 40-plus years of clinical experience I have yet to encounter another orthodontist who has the knowledge and understanding of mechanics that Dr. Renfroe possesses. He was peerless in his appreciation of anchorage.

"Dr. Renfroe did not *form* wires—he *sculpted* them," Dr. Haas continued. "What a treat for a student to observe those long deft fingers take a straight piece of round wire and, in three-to-five seconds, see it transformed into a perfect arch form with all the required characteristics."

As a fellow orthodontics professor at UIC, Dr. Cyril Sadowsky, said of Dr. Renfroe, "He wrote the book on technique—literally."

Earl Renfroe Leads the Battle for Acceptance of African-Americans in Dentistry

by Claude E. Driskell, DDS
University of Illinois at Chicago College of Dentistry
Class of 1954

A significant thought that was manifested by a discussion of black dentists in 1938 about the human and civil rights of black dental professionals was published in an old *Lincoln Dental Society Journal* dated January 1939. At a monthly seminar meeting of the society, its older members elected to share an analytical comparative cross-reference of how racism in 1938 affected the black dental professionals of the South and the North 73 years after the emancipation of 1865.

Surprisingly, the discussion revealed a seemingly self-contradictory fact—a paradox. In 1938, the old baggage of traditional racism, carried over from the past agricultural age, was very reluctantly giving way to the new industrial age and its philosophy of integration.

The Lincoln Dental Society, a professional association for African-American dentists, itself resulted from the segregated American Dental Association and its local counterpart, the Chicago Dental Society, not allowing black dentists to become members. The men present in the 1938 meeting represented many of the pioneers who had to confront and overcome racism and its sister obstacles of prejudice, discrimination, and segregation.

The *Journal* was the umbilical cord of communication between the organization and its members, conveying thoughts, grievances, goals, and purposes. It also was an outlet for the society's members to express their professional views, share knowledge, and discuss common problems.

Established in 1911, the society still exists today as a coordinating liaison in organized dentistry. Its membership is com-

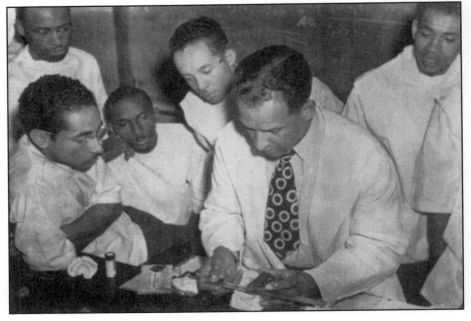

Dr. Renfroe led the battle for acceptance of African-Americans in dentistry.

posed of black dentists practicing in Chicagoland who earned their DDS degrees from dental schools all around the country.

The key figures in that 1938 discussion were dentists who graduated from dental school between 1904 and 1924, from such schools as Meharry, Howard, Northwestern, and the UIC College of Dentistry.

The discussion revealed that the Northern dental schools were only tokenly integrated. One-to-three percent of their students were black males, and they had no black females. Thus, the Northern schools technically satisfied the law in engaging in token integration, but surprisingly maintained segregation in their imposed discriminatory practice of keeping black dental students from working on white patients, and white students from working on black patients, in their clinical teaching facilities. That was the paradox: "segregated integration."

Society members therefore concluded that both Northern and Southern black dental students were experiencing segregation and discrimination. The difference was only in extent and degree.

The UIC College of Dentistry was no exception—until Dr. Earl W. Renfroe decided to make a difference.

Dr. Renfroe, dissatisfied with the conditions he had had to confront and endure as a dental student in the school, decided after he graduated that there had to be some changes for the sake of the black students who would attend the College in the future.

Perhaps in the times prior to 1931, Dr. Renfroe's year of graduation, it might not have been strategically wise to step forward, and no one had taken it upon himself to do so before Dr. Renfroe.

Courageously, in 1931 and 1932, Dr. Renfroe singlehandedly took it upon himself to challenge the faculty to change its policy of segregated dental clinics.

When recalling that Chicago at that time was referred to by the press as the most segregated city north of Dixie, one realizes

Dr. Claude E. Driskell (left) who had been a student of Dr. Renfroe (seated) in the 1950s, visits with his mentor four decades later.

the importance of Dr. Renfroe's decision.

The accomplishments of Dr. Renfroe in the field of dental education had their beginning in an atmosphere of racial inequality. He entered the College of Dentistry in 1927 as one of a token quota of "colored" students.

The College has existed as a teaching and training institution since 1892. It was not until the Class of 1904 that it graduated its first black dentist, W.C. Hobbs. Its second, W.T. Mitchell, graduated in 1908. Other blacks graduated in every year from 1909 to 1912, 1916 to 1919, 1923, 1924, 1926, 1928, and 1930, but never more than three in any year, and usually just one or two. By the time of Earl's graduation, only 20 blacks had preceded him in becoming College alumni.

Chicago's population in 1930 was seven percent black, but the dental school's population during the decade was only one-to-three percent black. In classes of an average 58-to-70 dental students, there usually were only one-to-three blacks. Some years had no black dental students.

Upon his entry to the school, he met black upperclassmen Silas Phillip Jones and Freeman Johnson Jr., the only two blacks in the 39-member Class of 1928. They informed him about the racial situation at the school.

B. Alleyne and G. Sneed were the other two black students in Earl's 1927 freshman dental class. In 1930 E. Wiggins graduated, but there were never more than six black students in the school between 1926 and 1931.

Until that latter year, when Dr. Renfroe's intervention began to turn things around, like at other dental schools, black students were not permitted to have white patients, and white students were not allowed to work on black patients.

But the number of black patients was increasing; blacks were migrating from Dixie to the West and South Sides of Chicago, more than doubling the 1920 recorded number of 109,458 blacks in the city to 233,903 by 1930.

So the school's clinic supervisor, Dr. Victor T. Nylander, asked recent graduate Dr. Renfroe to return to the school and take over a row of clinic chairs and to hire a fellow black dentist colleague if needed, to take care of the surplus black patients and earn a percentage of fees collected.

Dr. Renfroe recalled that this would have been a somewhat underhanded alternative to admitting more minority students, so he refused the offer. Instead, he asked why the enrolled white dental students couldn't take care of black, as well as white, patients. Many white students had told Dr. Renfroe that they wanted desperately to work on black patients—because there often were more black patients than white, and work without regard to race would allow the students to complete their required clinical work faster.

As an alternative to the offer, Dr. Renfroe agreed to accept a part-time position as a dental instructor to help find a favorable solution for the racial problem in patient admissions.

Dr. Renfroe would face faculty politics and resistance, but there was no turning back. Because of his concern that without constant observance the situation could reverse back to business as usual, he stayed on the job *without salary* for a number of years.

Eventually, prosthetic dentistry (now prosthodontics or restorative dentistry) became the first department to allow students to work on patients without regard to race. The chief of prosthetic dentistry, Dr. J.S. Kellogg, came to Dr. Renfroe and said, "I'm tired of all this racial stuff. The next Negro patient you get who needs dentures, send him or her to me. I'll see that a white student does the work." The other departments soon would follow prosthetics' lead.

As for an increase in black students, that too took time. In the 1940s, only five blacks graduated from the College, but in the 1950s, that number increased to 18 (including this author). The first black female, Barbara Cohn Howard, was admitted in 1970, and she eventually earned her DDS at Meharry. In 1975, Hollis Hunter Gibson became the first black female to graduate from the UIC College of Dentistry.

Since 1969, the University has become involved in an active recruitment/retention program to significantly increase the number of minority dental students at the College.

"Now it's an open school for anybody regardless of their color," Dr. Renfroe said in the late 1990s. "And I started it."

Contributions of Earl Renfroe to Pediatric Dentistry and to the Concept of Preventive Orthodontics

by Thomas K. Barber, DDS, MS
Professor Emeritus, University of California at Los Angeles
Former Professor and Head, Department of Pedodontics, University of Illinois at Chicago College of Dentistry

Since orthodontics was Dr. Earl Renfroe's forte, his contributions to the advancement of dental care for children have received less recognition than they have deserved.

My career as a pediatric dentist gathered a measure of notoriety in the application of orthodontic care in the younger child, but for that I can thank some strong influences by my mentors—including, in large part, the collegial efforts, support, and stimulation from Dr. Earl Renfroe on my behalf.

Dr. Renfroe and I collaborated in writing what is referred to as the seminal article on the concepts of preventive and interceptive orthodontics (Barber, T.K., and Renfroe, E., "Interceptive orthodontics for the general practitioner," *Journal of the American Dental Association*, 54(3): 328-347, 1957), which was re-published in many languages in several journals worldwide.

After more than 40 years of retrospection, Dr. Renfroe and I could say that this article, and our work that followed, produced considerable change in professional thinking and in the evolution of more modern clinical approaches to the guidance of the child's developing dentition.

I graduated from the College of Dentistry in 1949 and began specialty training in pediatric dentistry there. Around that time, Dr. Allan G. Brodie, dean and head of the Department of Orthodontics, conceived the need for a new predoctoral course in dental growth and development. Pairs of dental students would take annual dental records such as x-rays, dental casts, and oral exams of children in their pre-teens to enable the students to observe the changing dental development in these children throughout the period the dental student was in school. At

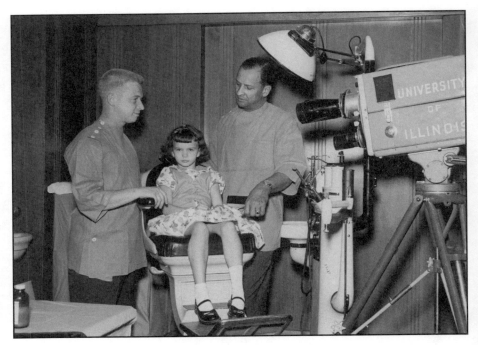

(Left to right) Dr. Thomas K. Barber and Dr. Earl W. Renfroe work with a young patient in front of a TV camera in the late 1950s.

the same time, the conduct of the course would allow the collection of valuable records, which could serve for future study and research in growth and dental development.

Dr. Brodie enlisted me in 1950 to accept a faculty appointment in the Department of Pediatric Dentistry and to lead this course. He made the comment to me that "one day in dental practice we will see others beside orthodontists providing orthodontic care, because the need is so great." He also said that there was much in dental malocclusion to be prevented that had not yet been defined.

Dr. Renfroe thought along the same lines. As early as 1948 and 1949, he presented several invited lectures entitled "Preventive Orthodontics" to professional societies. He also gave demonstrations on the ease of fabricating simple removable appliances using the then-new rapid curing acrylic materials.

As a postdoctoral student during 1949-50, I was invited to

serve as a part-time instructor in pediatric dentistry at Marquette University in Milwaukee. During my tenure there, Dr. Renfroe gave an invited lecture to the Department of Pediatric Dentistry on "Interceptive Orthodontics," which was later followed by a more general course given by the department on "Preventive Dentistry for Children" in which Dr. Renfroe participated. He repeated these invited presentations at many different venues over succeeding years; so Dr. Renfroe helped to plant within me a seed to nurture the topic within the field of pediatric dentistry.

Soon after, as a faculty member in pediatric dentistry at Illinois, I was invited by Dr. Brodie to be a participating guest in the preclinical training program given to advanced orthodontic graduate students. I was exposed to jaw growth and development, cephalometric analysis and the diagnosis and treatment planning of developing malocclusion, as well as the general principles of appliance design and clinic care of patients.

While Dr. Brodie conducted the theoretical seminars, Earl Renfroe was my constant mentor in the clinical application of concept. Indeed, he encouraged me to complete the clinical program with him so that I might be recognized as a board-eligible orthodontist. However, such was not my goal, as we had originally embarked upon my fuller understanding of malocclusions so that these concepts would be applied to the child younger than those seen by the orthodontist at the time. A study of how malocclusions develop in the younger child had never really been conducted.

Thus began a professional relationship between orthodontics and pedodontics (pediatric dentistry) that had never before existed and is rare even today. Until 1950, except to study normal growth, orthodontics had rarely approached the correction of malocclusion in children under the age of 12, or until the permanent dentition was complete in eruption. We therefore embarked on a long-term bi-clinical program to learn from each other.

Earl Renfroe became my colleague in pediatric dentistry. Together, along with other orthodontic and pedodontic faculty, we shared the knowledge of orthodontic technique and our knowledge of developing occlusions and malocclusions in young children. Together we viewed many clinical problems in youngsters, and stood by the chair to discuss how we might approach each one's particular situation so it got no worse.

We began to develop an expertise on what was correctable early and how to go about fixing it. By the mid-1950s, we felt quite confidant in the concepts we were developing and the clinical results that could be expected through their application.

Subsequently, Dr. Renfroe and I collaborated in the writing of that 1957 seminal *J.A.D.A.* article. With its publication was established an identity with the concept. Together and separately, Dr. Renfroe and I presented teaching sessions and discussions in print, in class, and on radio and television on the topics of prevention and early intervention of developing malocclusions in children.

Earl Renfroe approached the orthodontic discipline with the desire to look earlier at the younger child and to assist the pediatric dentist in providing earlier dental developmental care where indicated. At the same time, my pediatric dentistry approach was to elevate both the pediatric dental specialist and general practitioner to a higher level of care than that for which he or she had initially been trained.

Since 1957, the dental profession has witnessed considerable change in the early detection and prevention of many dental maladies. Especially with the recognition of deviations in normal jaw growth and following erratic dental development, the profession has made substantial strides in early detection and treatment provided to a broader population and by a broader professional base. It can be said that Dr. Earl Renfroe made a considerable contribution to children through his willingness to share his knowledge and experience with associated dental disciplines.

In time, both Dr. Renfroe and I each accepted burdens of departmental chairmanship; but that enhanced, rather than dampened, our mutual concern for the continuance of preventive care. While Dr. Renfroe was heavily engaged in the care and treatment of traditional orthodontic needs and in orthodontic education, he consistently gave of his knowledge to whatever professional group wished his counsel. He devoted those preventive efforts to the periodontal patient, to people with disabilities, and later to the care of the mature adult needing orthodontic correction. He was the consummate clinician.

Earl Renfroe also was remarkable in that he gave so much of himself to educational disciplines other than his own. Individuals involved in the general discipline of pediatric dentistry may not be aware of the benefits provided to children by Dr. Renfroe, but they are very great indeed.

It was my honor and pleasure to get to know him as I did—to study, work, and treat patients together, to share success in purpose, stature in profession, and contentment of accomplishment in retirement. I thank him deeply.

Home Life

by William S. Bike
Associate Director of Advancement and Alumni Affairs
University of Illinois at Chicago College of Dentistry

Dr. Earl W. Renfroe was fortunate to have had a partner in his journey of unparalleled accomplishment—his wife of almost 58 years, the former Hilda Forte.

"When Earl periodically entertained his students, Hilda provided a warm and gracious atmosphere in their home," recalled her sister, Mary F. Grady. "She also accompanied him on trips to Europe and on his numerous visits to Brazil," as well as to many other countries.

"In all of his interests and endeavors, she was a charming, cooperative, and supportive spouse," Mrs. Grady said.

Hilda was born in Barbados in the West Indies, one of four children in her family. "Our father died when I was very young, and my mother remarried a Barbadian living in Chicago," Hilda recalled. "I was the oldest girl. We came to the United States by boat when I was five, entering through Ellis Island in New York."

Growing up in Chicago, Hilda received her elementary, secondary, and college educations in the city. After graduation, she held administrative positions at Provident Hospital and the Illinois Federal Savings and Loan Association.

She met her husband through the UIC College of Dentistry in the late 1930s. "A dentist had extracted two of my teeth, but I needed further dental work and was sent to the College of Dentistry," Hilda remembered. "Earl was the consulting dentist on my case, and became my family's dentist."

Earl's interest in Hilda became more than professional. Once they were married, Hilda became as involved in all of her interests as Earl was in his. "During all of their years of marriage, Hilda was very active, being involved in the educational, cultural, and social activities of their children, and also serving as a volunteer in various organizations," Mrs. Grady said.

Some of those activities included the PTA, Jack and Jill of

Earl and Hilda Renfroe relaxing at the piano.

America, the National Conference of Christians and Jews (Hilda was Protestant co-chair of the Women's Board), the United Negro College Fund, the Women' s Board of the Chicago Urban League, the boards of trustees of Hull House and of the Fine Arts Quartet of Chicago, the presidency of the Bravo! Chapter of the Lyric Opera Guild, the vice presidency of the International Visitors Center, and Chicago Women's Travel. Hilda also occasionally worked in Earl's dental office, but also devoted her work time to travel consulting for Space Inc. Travel.

Hilda and Earl had two children, Diane Lynn Renfroe, now an attorney with Arthur Andersen in the Washington, DC-area, and Stephen Pilgrim Renfroe, a retired Air Force officer whose wife, Cheryl, is a physician. Hilda and Earl retired to Silver Spring, MD, in 1998 to live with Stephen and Cheryl and their children, Julia and Chase. Diane visited every weekend, and Earl Jr., Dr. Renfroe's son from his first marriage, kept in touch from Hawaii by phone, and visited from time to time.

Both through their accomplishments and graciousness, Hilda

and Earl became well known in Chicago society. Their home life was noteworthy enough to be one of the subjects of a *Chicago Tribune Magazine* article on March 16, 1969. The author wrote that in Chicago, there were "five key families in black society, among them the Renfroe" family.

The home Hilda provided meant the overextended Earl could indulge in some leisure time activities—ham radio operation, SCUBA diving, and more. Diane recalled that Earl was active in the Druids, a South Side Chicago social and business club for black men, and that his hobbies were those that required the Renfroe manual dexterity well-known to his dental students.

"He had a Jaguar XKE, and whenever he had free time he would work on it, and other cars, too," Diane said. "Jaguars needed a lot of maintenance, and he loved the mechanics. Anything related to working with his hands made him happy."

Another hobby was marksmanship. A UIC College of Dentistry faculty member recalls leaving a less-than-captivating

(Left to right) Hilda and Earl, and their children Diane and Stephen, in their up-to-date 1960s home.

Ham radio and SCUBA diving were two hobbies Earl Renfroe managed to squeeze into his busy lifestyle.

dental conference with Dr. Renfroe to get in some target shooting. "He hadn't picked up a gun in years, but he hit everything dead on," Dr. Renfroe's colleague recalled.

Everything they took on, it would appear, Earl and Hilda hit "dead on." In their final years, surrounded by family, Dr. and Mrs. Renfroe could bask in the memories of lives well lived.

When the time came, Death could not keep Earl and Hilda apart for very long. Hilda passed away on Sept. 13, 2000, and two months later on Nov. 14, Earl followed his beloved into eternity.

Reflections

by Claude E. Driskell, DDS
University of Illinois at Chicago College of Dentistry
Class of 1954

Dr. Earl Wiley Renfroe's overriding philosophy was simply, "do your best." "In all the stories we ever heard about him overcoming obstacles, that was the key message," said his daughter, Diane Renfroe.

Dr. Renfroe believed that in spite of the many recent triumphs of science and technology, man's basic inner nature has not kept up with his outer advances, and really has not changed significantly in the last 2,000 years. As a consequence, we must compel ourselves as a species to try even harder to learn from our human history. Our history is ourselves, evolving in time.

Dr. Renfroe felt that in our fast-growing industrialized civilization, man has created a system in which the human being is being utilized as a tool. This system results in too many competing for relatively too few jobs available. Unemployment always is a potential threat hovering over the heads of the workers—"labor"—an impersonal abstract.

Individualism has seemingly been gravely sacrificed by the quantity supply versus the actual need of labor, to be hired or fired as determined by the demand for the product. Such an atmosphere prefers a supply of labor larger than the demand for workers, which helps control those workers.

As the country transformed from agricultural to industrial from the middle of the 19th century through the 20th, increased population created both an increased labor force and escalated consumer demand, and theoretically a more prosperous society overall.

Dr. Renfroe predicted, because he has strong faith in humanity, that our great American system will prevail, regardless of the obstacles it will inevitably confront in the future.

He felt that this is a valued, significant system, essential, in the experiment of humanity, to our survival as a species. Can the species love itself? Can its members coexist? First, mankind has

Dr. Earl W. Renfroe in his 90s.

to learn to know itself before it can successfully learn to tolerate differences in its kind.

Dr. Renfroe saw our American system as a fundamentally democratic one, the world's first attempt to have many diverse races, colors, and religions co-exist in an amalgamated integration of harmonious compatibility.

The inherent spirit of both white and black America was more alike than different to Dr. Renfroe. Both historically resisted servitude by respective oppressors. Both have expressed the fiery nature to resist oppression in any fashion, and rose up to rebel whenever oppression was thrust upon them.

Historically, the transplanted African captives and their descendants in America have never passively and complacently accepted an imposed subordinate place in white America.

We, as one people, therefore must try to make live an idea. Henry Ford (1863-1947) once expressed, in a morale-boosting speech, that we might be directed to help solve our existing racial problems.

He said, "coming together is a beginning, and keeping together is a sign of progress, but actually deciding in our hearts to work together toward a common beneficial goal is true success!"

That was a philosophy by which Dr. Earl Wiley Renfroe lived his unique life.

Curriculum Vitae of Earl Wiley Renfroe

Born
January 9, 1907, Chicago, Illinois.

Died
November 14, 2000, Silver Spring, Maryland.

Family
Wife, Hilda Forte.
Children, Earl Jr., Diane L., Stephen P.

Education
James H. Bowen High School, 1921-25.
Crane Junior College, 1925-27.
University of Illinois at Chicago College of Dentistry, 1927-31
    (DDS).
University of Illinois at Chicago College of Dentistry, 1940-42
    (MS-Orthodontics).

Certifications
Illinois State Specialty Board, Orthodontics, 1946.
American Board of Orthodontics, 1955.

Licenses
Illinois, General Practice of Dentistry, 1932.
California, General Practice of Dentistry, 1946.
Barbados, West Indies, General Practice of Dentistry, 1977.

Teaching positions at the University of Illinois at Chicago
Instructor in Oral Diagnosis, 1933.
Instructor in the Infirmary, 1935-40.
Instructor in Orthodontics, 1946-47.
Assistant Professor, Orthodontics, 1947-53.
Associate Professor, Orthodontics, 1953-57.
Professor of Orthodontics, 1957-66.

Lecturer, Undergraduate Orthodontics
Juniors, 1963-66;
Freshmen, 1968-72.
Professor and Head of Orthodontics Department, 1966-73.
Medical Staff, University of Illinois at Chicago Hospital, 1972-73.
Professor Emeritus of Orthodontics, 1973-2000.

Professional memberships
American Association of Orthodontics, life member.
American Dental Association, life member.
Edward H. Angle Society of Orthodontics, senior member.
Chicago Association of Orthodontics, president, 1963-64.
Chicago Dental Society, life member.
Illinois State Society of Orthodontics, member.
Lincoln Dental Society, member.
Midwestern Society of Orthodontists, life member.
Orthodontic Alumni Association of the University of Illinois,
        member.
Sociedade Paulista de Ortodontia, socio honorário.

Civic organizations
Alpha Phi Alpha Fraternity.
American Radio Relay League, general operator, WB9SQE U.S.;
        8P6IF Barbados; AAV51K U.S. Army.
Chicago Council on Foreign Relations, vice president, 1968.
Chicago Natural History Museum.
Chicago Planetarium Society.
Chicago Urban League.
Cousteau Society.
The Druids.
International Oceanographic Foundation.
National Conference of Christians and Jews.
National Geographic Society.
National Rifle Association.
Pan American Society.
Sigma Pi Phi Fraternity, Beta Boule.
20 Fathom (SCUBA) Club .

Private dental practice
General dental practice, 1932-40.
Practice in orthodontics, 1946-75.
Consultant in orthodontics, 1975-2000.

Continuing education
Seminarian, Annual Midwest Seminar of Dental Medicine, Maxwelton Braes, Bailey's Harbor, Wisconsin, 1958-87.

Military service, U.S. Army, U.S. Army Reserves
Captain to Lieutenant Colonel, 1940-46.
Chief of Dental Service, Dental Corps #1, Ft. Huachuca, Arizona, 1943-45.
Colonel, Dental Corps, U.S. Army Reserves, 1958.
Colonel, Dental Corps, U.S. Army Retired Reserves, 1963.
Colonel, U.S. Army Retired Reserves, 1968.
Brigadier General, Illinois Army National Guard, 1984.

Hobbies
Amateur radio, general operator rating.
Aviation, first black commercial pilot, State of Illinois, and third in the United States.
Marksmanship, pistol and rifle.
Military affiliate radio system, U.S. Army.
Model locomotives.
SCUBA diving.
Sports car repair.

Travel
Visited: Antigua, Aruba, Australia, Bora Bora, Bermuda, France, Italy, Jamaica, Mexico, New Zealand, Portugal, Puerto Rico, St. Thomas, St. Vincent, Tahiti, Trinidad, Virgin Islands, Venezuela. Lectured in: Argentina, Barbados, Brazil, Canada, Colombia, England, Germany, Madeira, Peru.

Listings
Who's Who in the World.
Who's Who in America.
Who's Who in the Midwest.
Who's Who Amongst Black Americans.
Blue Book of London.
American Men of Science.
Dictionary of International Biography.
Wisdom Hall of Fame.

Honors, appointments, and offices
Chairman, Orthodontic Section, National Dental Association.
Consultant to Veterans Administration Hospital, Tuskeegee, Alabama.
Member, Program Committee, Chicago Association of Orthodontists.
Certificate from Meharry Medical College for service to Dental College, Nashville, Tennessee.
Elected to membership in Omicron Kappa Upsilon.

Member, Committee on Services for Crippled Children, Chicago Association of Orthodontists.
Grand Chairman, University of Illinois Orthodontic Alumni Reunion meeting.
Certification, American Board of Orthodontics.
Board of Censors, Chicago Association of Orthodontists.
Certificate, Uptown Dental Forum, for exemplary presentation.

Certificate, Associação Paulista de Cirurgiões Dentistas, São Paulo, Brazil, Seccao do Ortodontia for course on edgewise technique.
Fellowship, Illinois State Dental Society.
Dental Advisory Committee of Chicago Dental Society to Cook County Department of Public Aid.
Certificate, Sociedade Paulista de Ortodontia for course on edgewise technique.
Certificate, Associação Paulista de Cirurgiões Dentistas, São Paulo, Brazil, for paper given on "Extraction in Orthodontics."

Certificate, Faculdade de Farmacia e Odontologia for participation in dental seminar honoring Prof. Jorge Gonzales Dias, Ararquara, Brazil.

Member, Steering Committee of National Conference of Christians and Jews.

President-Elect, and President, Chicago Association of Orthodontists.

Certificate, Ia. Semana Piraciabana de Ortodontia for paper, "Ramificacoes de Problema Malocclusao."

Member, National Association on Standard Medical Vocabulary, Charleston, Indiana.

Fellowship, American College of Dentists.

Dr. Renfroe's *Technique Training in Orthodontics* made required reading by the Brazilian Army for its dentists.

Diploma, Sociedade Paulista de Ortodontia.

Member, Examining Committee of Illinois Orthodontic Alumni Reunion.

University of Illinois Orthodontic Alumni Association Meeting dedicated to Dr. Renfroe.

Certificate, Associacion Odontologica Argentina Escuela de Majoramiento Profesional for course on "Tenico de Arco de Canto," 20 sessions, Buenos Aires, Argentina.

Executive Committee, Chicago Association of Orthodontists.

Fellowship Award, Illinois State Dental Society.

Instructorship Award, UIC College of Dentistry, junior class.

Member, Public Relations Committee of Midwestern Society of Orthodontists.

Member, Executive Committee of Chicago Association of Orthodontists.

Foreign correspondent for *Bulletin of Paulista Sociedade Ortodontia de Brasil*.

Member, Board of Directors; and chair, Travel Committee; Chicago Council on Foreign Relations.

Member, University of Illinois Committee on Human Relations
and Equal Opportunity.
Member, Curriculum Committee, UIC College of Dentistry.

Member, Advisory Committee to Develop an Ephebodontics
Program, UIC College of Dentistry.
Elected member, Committee on Educational Policy, University
Senate, University of Illinois Professional Colleges.
Elected member, Executive Committee, UIC College of
Dentistry.
Vice-President, Toastmasters' Club, Medical Center Chapter.

Consultant in orthodontics, Illinois State Specialty Board
Examiners.
Member, Committee on International Personnel, University of
Illinois.
Certificate of Recognition, Tri-County Dental Assistants Society,
for contributions to education.
Diploma, Guanabara Section, Brazilian Dental Association, for
giving course in orthodontics.
Certificate from Congresso Odontologico Riograndense, Porto
Alegre, Brazil.

Certificate of Recognition, Chicago Dental Assistants
Association.
Program Chair, 33rd Annual Meeting, Midwestern Society of
Orthodontists.
Certificate, Paulistano Society of Ortodontia, São Paulo, Brazil.
Certificate of Appreciation, Washington State Dental Society.
Certificate, American Academy of Orthodontia for the General
Practitioner.

Key to the City, presented by the Mayor of Lima, Peru.
Diploma, 3rd Congreso Americano de Las Diagnacias for pre-
senting course in interceptive orthodontics, Lima, Peru.
Certificate of Appreciation, Orthodontic Alumni Association,
UIC College of Dentistry.

Certificate for participation in Seminario International de
    Ortodontia, Congresso Brasileiro de Ortodontia, and
    Congresso Paulista de Ortodontia, São Paulo, Brazil.
Distinguished Alumnus Award, UIC College of Dentistry
    Alumni Association.

Member, Chicago Senior Citizens Hall of Fame.

Clinics, courses, and lectures given at
Akron Dental Society, Akron, OH.
Alpha Omega Alumni Chapter, Milwaukee, WI.
American Academy of Orthodontics for General Practitioners,
    Racine, WI.
American Association of Orthodontists, San Francisco, CA;
    Boston, MA; Chicago, IL.
American Society of Dentistry for Children, Chicago, IL.

Associacao Paulista de Cirurgioes Dentistas, São Paulo, Brazil.
Associacion Odontologia, Buenos Aires, Argentina.
    Barbados.
Brazilian Dental Association, Guanabara, Brazil.
Brazilian Dental Society of Riograndense, Porto-Alegre, Brazil.

California Pedodontic Research Conference, Santa Barbara, CA.
Central Association of Orthodontists, St. Paul, MN.
Chicago Dental Assistants' Society, Chicago, IL.
Chicago Dental Society, Chicago, IL.; Northside Branch;
    Midwinter Meeting.
Colombia.

Congress Americanos de las Diagnacias, Lima, Peru.
Congresso Brasileiro de Ortodontia, São Paulo, Brazil.
Congresso Paulista de Ortodontia, São Paulo, Brazil.
Councilor District Dental Society, Green Bay, WI.
Dade County Dental Society, Madison, WI.

Dixon School, Chicago, IL.

Commonwealth Dental Society, Newark, NJ.

Edward H. Angle Society of Orthodontists, Indianapolis, IN; Chicago, IL; Los Angeles, CA; Midwestern Component; California Component.

England.

Essex County Dental Society, East Orange, NJ.

European Orthodontic Society, Garmisch-Partenkirchen, Germany.

427th General Hospital, Fort Sheridan, IL.

Genesee District Dental Society, Flint, MI.

Howard University, Washington, DC.

International Academy of Orthodontics, Central Section, Chicago, IL; New York, NY.

Joliet Dental Study Group, Joliet, IL.

Lincoln Dental Society, Chicago, IL.

Loma Linda University, Loma Linda, CA.

Madeira.

Marquette University, Milwaukee, WI.

McCoste Public School, Chicago, IL.

Meharry Medical College, Nashville, TN.

Middle Atlantic Pedodontic Study Club, Philadelphia, PA.

Milwaukee Dental Society, Milwaukee, WI.

National Dental Association, Indianapolis, IN; Chicago, IL.

Northwestern University, Chicago, IL.

Provident Hospital, Chicago, IL.

St. Edmond's School, Chicago, IL.

São Paulo State Orthodontic Society, Pirachicaba, Brazil; São Paulo, Brazil.

Semana Odontologia in Araraguara, Brazil

Seminario International de Ortodontia, São Paulo, Brazil.

Sociedade Paulista de Ortodontia, São Paulo, Brazil.

Tri-County Dental Assistants' Society, Oakbrook Center, IL.

University of Illinois at Chicago College of Dentistry;
UIC Medical Center; UIC Orthodontic Alumni Association;
UIC Sanders Dental Research Study Club, Chicago, IL.
University of Toronto, Toronto, Canada.

Upsala College, East Orange, NJ.
Uptown Dental Forum, Chicago, IL.
Will-Grundy County Dental Society, Joliet, IL.

Articles published in
American Journal of Orthodontics.
Anais de l Semana Piracicabana de Ortodontia.
Angle Orthodontist.
Chicago Bulletin of the Lincoln Dental Society.
Journal of the American Dental Association.
Ortodontia.
Trans European Orthodontic Society.
Year Book of Dentistry.

Books
Technique Training in Orthodontics.
Edgewise.
Edgewise (Japanese edition).

Biographies of essayists

Thomas K. Barber, DDS, MS, earned his DDS and histology MS degrees from the University of Illinois at Chicago College of Dentistry in 1949. He served on the faculty from 1950 to 1969, leaving with the rank of professor and having served as the head of the Department of Pedodontics from 1965 to 1969. A former Fulbright scholar, he launched the pediatric dentistry program at the University of California at Los Angeles, where he is professor emeritus.

William S. Bike, associate director of advancement and alumni affairs at the University of Illinois at Chicago College of Dentistry, is the editor of the College's *Alumni Report* magazine and the author of two books, *Streets of the Near West Side* and *Winning Political Campaigns.* He is a former writer for *Dental Products Report* magazine.

Paulo Affonso de Freitas, DDS, earned his dental degree in 1951 at the University of São Paulo, and did his graduate work in orthodontics at the University of Pennsylvania. The founder and former president of the São Paulo State Orthodontic Society, he also was president of the first Brazilian Orthodontic Meeting in 1957. Dr. Freitas also is the founder and former president of the International College of Dentists' District Brazil, and founder and former director of the journal *Ortodontia.* He practices in São Paulo.

Claude E. Driskell, DDS, is a 1954 graduate of the University of Illinois at Chicago College of Dentistry. He has practiced general dentistry on the South Side of Chicago for more than 45 years. Dr. Driskell is active in several dental organizations, including the Lincoln Dental Society. An avid historian and writer, Dr. Driskell is the author of the book *Chicago Black Dental Professionals: 1850-1983,* published in 1982.

Bruce S. Graham, DDS, MS, MEd, is dean of the University of Illinois at Chicago College of Dentistry. He previously served as dean of the University of Detroit-Mercy School of Dentistry. The recipient of many awards, Dr. Graham earned the Wolverine Dental Society Award for Support and Accomplishments in Minority Student Recruitment and Retention 1997. He is the author of more than a dozen papers and has given many research presentations in the United States and Canada.

Ronald A. Ramsay, BDS, Cert. Orth., completed primary and secondary education in Barbados; graduate dental training in Bristol, England, where he was awarded a medal for excellence in clinical dentistry; and postgraduate training at the Eastman Dental Centre in Rochester, NY. Dr. Ramsay practices in Barbados and is a member of the Caribbean Society of Orthodontists, the American Association of Orthodontists, and the World Federation of Orthodontists. He and his Colombian-born wife, Marlene, are the parents of Rafael, Natasha, and Jonathan.

Col. Earl Renfroe Jr. earned his B.A. in education from the University of Nebraska. He entered the United States Air Force as a Private in 1951, retiring in 1982 with the rank of Colonel. Completing his pilot training at Greenville, MS, and Enid, OK, he flew 35 combat missions during the Korean Conflict and 107 in the Vietnam War. Col. Renfroe was twice awarded the Legion of Merit, received the Air Medal five times, and also earned the Distinguished Flying Cross.

Mark J. Valentino, assistant dean for advancement and alumni affairs at the University of Illinois at Chicago College of Dentistry, has been in charge of development for the College since 1991. During his tenure, the College of Dentistry surpassed its $8.2 million *Campaign Illinois* fundraising goal, realizing gifts in excess of $11 million. He also is the editor and publisher of the *Near West/South Gazette*, the community newspaper serving the UIC neighborhood. In 1997, Valentino was honored by the

94

Chicago Commission on Human Relations for his community service.

Photo credits